REAR
PRACTICAL TOO̶ ̶GENIUS

To Chris,

Thank you for your support. May you tap into the inner teacher in you and unleash all the genius around you. ~~Stay~~ strong, stay the course. Keep shining

YENNENGA ADANYA

ISBN: 978-1508502951

Cover Illustration Copyright © 2015
Cover design by Crystal Goodwin & Will Starks
Cover art by Will Starks
Editing by Raina Turner

For bulk orders call 678-429-0107
Available online at yennengaadanya@gmail.com

TABLE OF CONTENTS

ACKNOWLEDGEMENTS

I want to first acknowledge all of the master teacher ancestors who came before us whose knowledge and inspiration keeps me going. I would be remiss if I didn't give thanks to my son Akinwole who is my joy and inspiration and Dr. Asa G. Hilliard, III who was the educator who unleashed the genius in me. I also would like to acknowledge my parents who put up with my very creative, and sometimes scattered mind, my dada, Afia Raina, who always encourages me to trust my genius in times of doubt, Erika Bullock a fellow member of the Urban Education Think Tank at Georgia State University who unleashed the writer in me and has been a cheerleader throughout this process, Chike Akua who has been my consistent accountability partner in completing this book urging me to stop running from what he deemed a calling, and Baba Mwalimu K. Bomani Baruti whose work has a major influence on the way I teach and the way I rear my child. I thank my ADOFO family, who has become my own personal community and all of the people who have supported me throughout the years including the families and communities who have entrusted me with the well being of their children. Lastly, I want to acknowledge a true god-sent, Gary Black, who has been that last bit of inspiration I needed to birth this baby.

INTRODUCTION

**Throughout this work you will see Africa spelled with a "K". When I say
Afrikan, I am referring to melanated people. Additionally, I choose to spell
Africa with a "K" to symbolize our need to return to our original selves as an
Afrikan people, a whole.*

The inspiration for this book came from my experience as a parent
and teacher. Whatever I am called to do, I like to do it well and get
results. I found myself almost obsessing about mastering the art of
teaching and parenting. I aspired, and expected, to unleash, within
the children under my care, the same genius that our ancestors
possessed. These same traits are those that created, developed, and
invented world wonders, still admired to date, like the pyramids and
the ancient temples. Whenever I found myself having a difficult time
teaching my students or rearing my son I would not rest until I found
solutions.

I have always felt like every child is a genius and it is my role as a
teacher and a parent to unleash and nurture that genius. In doing so,
I could effectively counter an environment that consistently placed
Afrikan children in a box, a box that is foreign, unnatural and
ultimately isn't suitable for their successful development.

Fresh off a riveting speaking engagement, a colleague of mine asked
me what the title of my presentation was. "How to Survive Public
School as an Afrikan Child" I told her. Intrigued, but clearly
frustrated, she asked why the book had to be just for Afrikan
children. I explained to her that the key thing to understand was
that Afrikan people, as all people, have specific distinctions when it
comes to learning, innate behaviors, core values, and spirituality.
Afrikans are creative, hands-on, deep-thinkers, yet everything about
the American education they are subjected to is anti-Afrikan.

As I shared this knowledge with parents and students alike, I was
constantly reminded to put my experiences and advice on paper by
the parents who basically begged for it and by those who have met
my son or some of the children I've worked with over the years. I

have done presentations for years from county to county, state to state, providing consultation, guidance, and tips on how to rear a genius. This is ultimately what this book encompasses, my secrets to unleashing the genius in Afrikan children, youth, and even adults.

America's public schools are intellectual wastelands and have been so since their initial establishment. Public schools across the nation are suffocating the intellectual capacity of Afrikan child. Children have the expectation level equivalent to robots barring any deviation from the consistently ineffective curriculum imposed by public schools. To make matters worse, recess has been taken away, ADHD diagnoses are being thrown around like candy, Afrikan children are being placed in special education classes at an alarming rate, and the teachers and administrators are unenthused (oftentimes not even believing that the children they teach can actually succeed). These same 'educators' sit around in teacher's lounges bashing the students, parents, administration, and community while collecting their checks and ultimately leaving the children to waste away intellectually and spiritually.

It is sickening to walk through most urban schools across the nation. The schools look like prisons and you are oftentimes welcomed at the door by an armed police officer directing you through a metal detector. When walking down the prison-like hallways, you can hear teachers yelling at the students, you see teachers and students off-task staring into their cell phones or the computer, students with earplugs in their ears, and teachers congregating in the hallways leaving their class unsupervised. I could go on forever. The bottom line is, when entering most public schools you see everything but education occurring.

Contrary to popular belief, the academic content is the least bit of the problem that prevents students from succeeding. The problem is the child's negative environment, which affects the way they view themselves, their values and expectations. In order to succeed, your child must want to and believe that he or she can. Many times this desire to succeed is not instilled in students subjected to anti-Afrikan environments.

In Western society, and across the diaspora, Afrikan children are consistently bombarded with negative views and images of themselves. By the age of eight children have heard and understand the phrase "achievement gap". It is spoken of so much in schools, news, and in the home that it enters their vocabulary. Rather than presenting beautiful, young minds with high potential, the mass media portrays our children as thugs and perpetuates the notion that they can only achieve success by being in the music, entertainment, or sports industry.

The music on the radio and on television romanticizes drug dealing, stripping, domestic violence, misogyny, promiscuity, individualism, and capitalism. The effect of these constantly portrayed messages by mainstream society is more damaging than people seem to believe. It robs the children of their Afrikan spirit, mind, and ultimately their soul.

Countless times I have been in a situation where a parent reached out for help with their student (usually complaining that their child is failing in school and they are at their wits end with them). I would meet with the child and could immediately see the defeat in their eyes. It was written all over them. During the consultation, all I (and the child) heard were negative things about their academic, behavior, sentiment, and attitude. The child sat quietly taking every blow delivered by their beloved parent(s). These same parents are considered the child's first teachers and should be the ones uplifting and affirming their greatness.

Concerned for their child's intellectual well being in a system that is ultimately designed for their failure, they acquiesce to the status quo's methodology, separating parenting from education, and they give up their power as parents. At this point the parents are extremely frustrated and the child no longer believes that they can actually achieve. Sadly, the child believes the same. They no longer feel there is any amount of effort they can put forth to render success. Their parents are disappointed in them, their teachers do not seem to like them, their peers believe that they are "slow" and ridicule them for being on "Level I", and tragically they are disappointed in themselves. These children often resign to doing just enough to keep their parents and teachers off their backs (if that) and hope for a passing grade.

As a result, the reaction by their peers and parents is oftentimes hostile and diminishing, forgetting that children are people/human too. The child would much rather succeed than fail. However, the effort that they put forward to accomplish the goals and expectations, many times set for them, is underestimated or overlooked all together.

A lot of the time spent with my clients was undoing the damage done to them in both their home/community environment and the public school system. I had to teach them to see and appreciate exactly what I saw in them, a genius. I would constantly remind them that they were genius, showed them examples of geniuses, what genius behavior looked like and had them compare the characteristics found to their own character traits. I would also take the same characteristics these students exhibited, that many adults in their lives perceived to be negative, and translate them positively.

For instance, the child who always rebelled, talked back, questioned everything, and would argue their teacher down; I would emphasize how those qualities would greatly benefit a lawyer. If they doodled during class or tagged walls (graffiti) in the community, I would emphasize how much of an artist they were. Not only would I tell them these things, but I would also show them examples and role models who possessed similar traits. I exposed these children to as many positive images and examples that were direct reflections of them. With constant reinforcement of (high) expectations, incentive programs and consequences, slowly but surely the confidence level of my students (clients) increased.

This elevated confidence level was extremely key to their progress. Without the confidence of their ability to succeed, working with them was virtually impossible. Students wouldn't receive any instruction from me and they would not put any effort towards the goals. Increasing their confidence was never an easy task. What I found was many times the student harbored a lot of hurt and resentment, which was projected on me. There were many times where I would have to love them through tantrums or talk them into trusting themselves, but my perseverance was necessary for their success. The worse thing you can do is 'throw in the towel'.

As an educational consultant, many of the students that I have worked with over the years improved tremendously once they believed that they could. The greatest intellectual achievements in the history of man have been from Afrikan people. How is it that we now have the largest population of children in Special Education, diagnosed with learning disabilities and discarded as intellectually incapable of even meeting the expectations of a system of low expectations? It is disheartening to say the least.

As the parent of a young genius, I refuse to believe that our babies are not capable of achieving at the height of their ancestors if not greater. Dr. Asa G. Hilliard, III proclaimed, and I emphatically believe, there are no Afrikan children in any group who are not genius. There is no secret on how to teach them; treat them like humans and love them. With this as my teaching philosophy I have been blessed to unleash the genius in hundreds of children across the nation. From the child reading on a Pre-K level in the 3rd grade, to the high school student ready to drop out, I have been able to inspire young Kings and Queens to be Afrikan, to be their ancestors in spirit and in truth, to be geniuses.

Rearing a genius is no easy plight, especially in this world full of distractions, contradictions, and hypocrisies. One of the most important factors is controlling the child's environment. This book outlines various ways that parents can create an environment (physical, mental, and spiritual) that can nurture the genius in their child. Believe it or not, a child's environment plays a key role in shaping their reality. A child environment has the potential to either build them up or destroy them. It is my hope that this book will be provide effective strategies to use in your efforts to rear your child well.

This book has been broken up into three sections. Chapters 1-8 offer advice and strategies on how to develop a productive home environment that is conducive for rearing a genius, Chapters 9 – 10 outline how to support your child schooling, and Chapter 11 outlines the importance of community involvement, how to build your own personal community and how to stay involved.

As you explore this work I have compiled for your child's success inside and out of the classroom, I encourage you to reflect on this quote from Dr. Asa G. Hilliard, III (Nana Baffour), an ancestor who I hold near and dear to my heart and who resides in my spirit. "In our (Afrikan) worldview, our children are seen as divine gifts of our creator. Our children, their families, and the social and physical environment must be nurtured together. They must be nurtured in a way that is appropriate for a spiritual people, whose aim is to 'build for eternity'."

DEVELOPING MASTER STUDENTS

In my experience as an educator, I've observed a major deficit in the world of academia that poses a fundamental challenge to student success. The rising generation—brought up on the Internet and advanced technology—displays a severe lack of some of the essential student skills needed to successfully matriculate through their academic career. Students are missing many of the following must-have skills of an effective learner:

- Note Taking Skills
- Organization Skills
- Networking Skills
- Questioning and Analytical Skills, and
- Communication Skills

Unbelievably so, these student skills are rarely taught in school. Additionally, there aren't any formal, required standards that address master student skills. Students are often expected to naturally know how to navigate schooling, one of the most unnatural processes of their lives.

Throughout my educational career there are few times where I remember a teacher purposefully planning and teaching students basic, yet crucial, skills needed for student success i.e. how to take notes, how to use their notes to complete homework, how to organize their notebooks and lockers, how to manage both their classroom and study time, how to independently search for resources, the purpose of a highlighter and how to use it effectively, and how to assess their progress.

While studying under Dr. Asa G. Hilliard, III, world-renowned educator and black psychologist, I learned the concept of master learners. These learners are problem solvers who consistently ask questions, seek knowledge, engage in deep thought (critical thinking), and apply knowledge.

Dr. Hilliard proclaimed all children are genius and individuals seeking to become master learners could practice and perfect their student skills. Successful practice and perfection of these skills would increase the amount of information the student could learn in a shorter amount of time. Until that time, I had never considered that one could perfect the art of being a student, but it made perfect sense; you can master anything if you consciously make the effort. I had struggled my entire academic career to constantly achieve at the highest level possible. There I was in graduate school, seeking to become a teacher, and no one had ever taught me how to make the effort to master learning.

Once taught how to master my student skills, it unleashed the master student (turned scholar) in me and ultimately contributed to advancing my skills as a master teacher once I entered the classroom. From that point on, learning behaviors and student skills were a consistent component of all of my lessons. I created learning behavior standards and objectives and added them to the list of standards that I taught throughout the school year. These revised standards had a great impact on my students' achievement levels. My average C students elevated to A and B students and my A and B students found it easier to sustain high achievement.

What many parents fail to realize, and are sometimes intimidated by, is the fact many of these skills can, and in many cases must, be taught at home. Rest assured, it is not necessary for parents to be rocket scientists to be able to teach these skills. Parents can simply reflect on the skills/practices that helped them be successful in school, or some the strategies they used to be successful throughout their careers. If neither of these options proves to be helpful, with this being the age of information, parents can always do a bit of research on their own. There is a plethora of literature readily available in most local bookstores and online that outlines strategies and skills that have proven to be effective.

Provided below is a list of tips on how students can develop master student skills. These are strategies that have proven to work for me over the years as a parent and teacher. I found it extremely beneficial to post these tips on the wall of my classroom and provide it as a document for parents and students to refer to often. Share these strategies with your child. Read through the tips with them. Have them to identify those that they think would help them. As your child begins to use the strategies and make the effort to perfect their students skills, be sure to provide praise when due. Children love praise!

Note Taking Skills

Adequate notes are a necessary aide to efficient studying and learning in school. Copy the tips below and give to your child(ren). Reinforce the following suggestions and encourage your child to consistently work on their note taking system where needed:

- Listen actively. If possible, take the time to think before you write – but be cautious if the writing assignment is timed, you don't want to get too far behind.

- Develop and use a standard method of note taking, like Cornell Notes, including punctuation, abbreviations, margins, etc.

- Take and keep notes in a large notebook. A large notebook allows you to adequately indent and use an outline format.

- Leave a few spaces blank as you move from one point to the next so that you can fill in additional points later if necessary. Your objective is to take helpful notes, not to save paper.

- Do not try to take down everything that the teacher says. It is impossible, and unnecessary, to do so because everything is not of equal importance. Spend more time listening and attempt to take down the main points. If you are writing as fast as you can, you cannot be as selective a listener. There may be some times, however, when it is more important to write than to think. For instance, around test time teachers tend to provide an abundance of verbal and written information. Capture all of the information and ask questions later.

- Listen and look for key points (they tend to follow phrases like, "...be sure to focus on..." or "one of the main things we will focus on this week will be..."), transitions from one point to the next, repeat of points for importance, changes in voice inflections, listing of a series of points ("first, second, third..."), etc.
- Many teachers attempt to present a few major points and several minor points in a lesson. The rest is explanatory material and samples. Try to listen for the main points and avoid getting lost in the minor points. Be alert for cues (mentioned above) on what the teacher thinks is important.

- Make your notes legible enough for your own reading and use abbreviations i.e. msg vs. message or ex. vs. example. Keep in mind: although good penmanship is a necessary, it should not hinder you from capturing important information.

- Copy everything written on the board. Some of the notes may seem unimportant, but if you copy it, it may serve as a useful tool for you (or your parents) later. Sufficient notes tend to come in handy when you need to answer difficult homework or complete projects.

- When possible, sit as close to the front of the class as possible – there are fewer distractions and it is easier to hear, see, and attend to important material.

- Be sure to write down your assignments or teacher suggestion accurately – ask questions if you're not sure.

Organization Skills

A disorganized student is often described as forgetful and messy. They have a hard time keeping track of their materials and using their time efficiently. These students tend to have messy desks and repeatedly forget their homework. The simplest of tasks can baffle a disorganized student. This lack of organizational skills can be easily fixed by providing students with a few strategies to keep them on track.

There are tools and skills that students can use to manage their obligations and lead an organized life. Use the following tips to help disorganized students become organized and learn how to manage their responsibilities[1]:

Discuss the lack of organization you have observed

- The first thing that must be done is to have a candid conversation with the young person about how their lack of organization is negatively impacting their academic and/or personal life. Explain specifically how it is interfering with their progress in school and in life. For example: "The reason why you do not do well on your homework and quizzes is because you lose your notebook every other week."

The child will need assistance organizing his/her life

- Do not make the mistake of thinking your child knows how to effectively organize. You will have to teach them. Start by helping your child to reorganize their desk, class notebooks, and their bedroom. If necessary, purchase new notebooks or desk and closet organizers so that everything has its place. Be certain they have a pencil pack for their desk and a laundry hamper for their room, within easy reach. If you have previously tried these things to no avail, remind yourself that your child isn't deliberately trying to disobey

---

[1] Cox, Janelle. "Tips For Teachers To Help Disorganized Students." 5 Tips to Help the Disorganized Student: Help Organize the Disorganized. About.com. Web. 11 Feb. 2015.

you. He/she really doesn't know how to organize their belongings. It will take time, persistence and patience, but you will both get results.

A planner is a must

- Purchase a daily planner for your child and encourage them to use it every day. As the week progresses, the planner should include homework assignments, studying for tests, free time, time for meals, and so forth. Check in with your child(ren) at least once per week to review their planner. Provide reprimand when due, but be sure to equally provide praise when due as well.

Put a schedule on the disorganized student's wall or closet door

- Establishing a routine is invaluable for disorganized students. This gives students a sense of structure and they feel less frustrated once they know their expectations. Be sure to provide students with a class and home schedule they can reference throughout the day. Place their class schedule in their take-home folder, tape it onto their desk, and ask their teachers to post it in the classroom. Place their home schedule on their bedroom wall, on the living room wall, and on the refrigerator. By making the schedule visible and accessible, it will lessen the student's confusion of what is expected of them. Every household is unique, however, be sure your schedule includes homework time, a checklist of chores, reading time, selection of clothes for the next day, bedtime, morning wakeup time, and other tasks/activities related to their weekly routines. The child should also be involved in deciding what should be included in the schedule. This will help them take greater ownership of their responsibilities and hold themselves more accountable.

Have everything prepared for school before bedtime

- The student *must* collect all that is needed to walk out of the door in the morning. They should gather books, papers, notebooks, and writing instruments, put them neatly in their book bag and place them outside the bedroom door or at the front door. If there is a completed homework assignment due the next day or special items that they plan to take, be sure that this is inside of their book bag the night before. Students should also be sure to have their coats or jackets, caps, gloves, scarf, and umbrella ready if necessary (if the child is old enough, have them watch the news to check the weather report before school). This will eliminate many frantic mornings of last-minute searches.

Be very specific

- Establish expectations for neatness and other organizational skills. For example, don't tell a disorganized student to "clean out your desk" or "clean up your room." Be more specific. Perhaps say, "I want you to remove all the crumpled papers from your desk and put them in the trash." When that assignment is completed, explain what should be done next.

Clean out the clutter

- It is necessary for parents to do regular check-ins at their child's school. Disorganized students tend to have very messy desks. They may not ever voluntarily choose to clean it out, so it is up to you to set aside time each day or week for them to do so. Show them specific ways of how to keep their desks tidy. For example, throw away old assignments and materials they no longer use or place small items such as pencils and scissors in a container. Doing so will give them the skills they need to maintain an organized life and manage their responsibilities.

Monitor all schoolwork

- This tip goes hand-in-hand with parental support. Be sure to check for homework each night. Check their planner/agenda to make sure that they are writing down all of their homework daily. Check in with the teacher to make sure the student is completing their classwork and turning in homework, as well as, other at-home assignments. This will ensure that your student is staying on track. If your child is slacking on their work, be sure to develop consequences and stick to them. This will encourage students to be responsible for their belongings.

Enlist reinforcement and support from teacher(s) and other responsible adults in the student's life

- Parent-teacher communication is essential when you are dealing with a student who has poor organizational skills. Have teachers keep you in the loop daily, or weekly, by notifying you on your child's progress. Having the teacher's support will show the student that you mean business and both you and the teacher are working as a team to help him/her become self-sufficient.

Create a checklist

- Clearly define expectations by creating a checklist. This is truly the best tool to help students visually see what they need to accomplish and stay on track. Show students how to prioritize their list and check tasks off as they complete them. Once you reach the end of your list, a reward, in the form of praise, will positively encourage future completion of tasks.

Use memory aids

- Memory aids are a great way to help disorganized students remember their tasks and class materials. Provide your student with aids such as sticky notes, rubber bands, watches and timers. Have them tape checklists and class schedules to their folders and desks. Teach students acronyms to help them remember what to bring to school i.e., CATS (C=Carry, A= Assignment, T=to, S=School) or PANTS (P=Parent, A=Assignment, N=Notebook, T=Textbook, S=School).

Use the buddy system

- Enlist the help of an <u>organized</u> classmate or friend to remind the disorganized student of important tasks and student expectations. Only pair the student up with a shown responsible student that you can trust to help them out when you are busy or absent.

Label and color code everything

- The best way to keep students organized is to label and color-code all of their materials. Students who have a lack of organizational skills may feel overwhelmed when their materials are all over the place. Having specific colors for each subject will help students find assignments quickly and effortlessly.

Use praise as a reward

- When the disorganized student has shown improvement, be sure to compliment generously. All of us enjoy compliments, but for those who rarely receive them this is even more important.

Networking Skills

What is networking and how is it relevant in your student's academic career before college? If you have ever heard the saying, "It is not just what you know, it is also who you know!" you can begin to imagine the relevancy for your child at an early age. Networking is simply building mutually beneficial relationships and discussing topics that are of joint interest, no ages barred.[2]

Every time you make a new contact you are effectively tapping into a new circle of people, gradually building a list of contacts from various backgrounds. This concept is common in business but is typically not considered for school age (especially high school) students, though it is very beneficial to master this skill early.

Networking skills for school age students are skills that help students build and sustain sound relationships with their schoolteachers, administrators, and other influential adults in their lives. Some tips for successful student networking are as follows:

- Have students introduce themselves to all of their teachers. They can go a step further and request a "get to know you" meeting with the teacher at the beginning of the semester.

- Take the initiative to identify adults in the building who would be a great resource according to their academic needs and interest. For example, if a student is interested in a career in Journalism, even if they are not currently in the Journalism class, they should 1) introduce themselves to the teacher(s), 2) let them know that they are highly interested in becoming a Journalist and 3) ask the teacher if they could provide resources for self-study and/or participate in some of the current class activities or projects.

- Take the initiative to speak to the teacher about aspirations, strengths, and areas in need of improvement. This will help

[2] "Developing Networking Skills." *Developing Networking Skills*. Brunel University London, 29 Sept. 2014. Web. 11 Feb. 2015.
<http://www.brunel.ac.uk/services/pcc/students/finding-a-job/developing-networking-skills>

teachers to better understand the student and more accurately grade/measure their progress. Teachers also love students who are engaged in the process of learning and not merely participants.

- Take the initiative to get to know the counselor and other individuals in the school who control the supplemental resources available to the students. This will provide the student with information about various clubs, organizations, and resources that will support their needs and aspirations.

Ultimately networking for school age students is very similar to the networking adults should do throughout their career. Learning these skills and strategies early will increase the chances of them being able to accomplish what they will as they matriculate throughout not only their academic career, but throughout life. Encouraging and teaching these skills to students not only improves their ability to better position themselves in school and beyond graduation, but it also give parents an opportunity to sharpen their networking skills as well.

Questioning and Analytical Skills[3]

Developing inquiry (questioning and answering) skills may not seem like it would require much effort, but you will be surprised at the results good questioning yield compared to weaker inquiries. We all know it isn't what you say, it's how you say it. The same thing can be said about one's ability to analyze questions directed towards them. Understanding one's intent or what it is they are looking for is a valuable skill that is constantly underdeveloped in adults and children alike. When you approach questioning and answering skills, be sure to answer children's questions in a way that promotes deep (critical) thinking.

Deep (critical) thinking is on a thought level higher than merely memorizing facts or repeating something back to someone exactly the way it was told to you. When students think critically they take thinking beyond restating the facts they think of how they can apply those facts — understand them, build onto their prior knowledge, connect them to other facts and concepts, categorize them, manipulate them, put them together in new or innovative ways, and apply them as they seek new solutions to new problems.

Parents can do a lot to encourage critical thinking, even when they are answering children's questions. Families play a significant role encouraging critical thinking with their young children and teens, even when having a casual conversation. Asking open-ended questions that don't have one "right" answer gives children confidence to respond in creative ways without being afraid of being "wrong." After reading a book together, a parent might ask their child a question such as: "If you were that character, how would you have persuaded Woodrow to turn himself in?" rather than something like "What was the main character's name in the book?"

Below are more examples of questions to ask your child to spark discussion, make them think critically, and encourage deep thinking[4].

When reading a book, ask:

"What do you think might happen next?"
"Does this remind you of anything from your life?"
"Can you tell me about what you read today?"
"Why did he/she act that way?"
Does this book remind you of others that you have read?

When visiting an unfamiliar place, ask:

"How is _____ similar to/different from _____?"
"Can you explain/show me that in another way?"

When making an important decision:
"How would you rank _____?"
"How do you imagine _____ would look?"
"What do you think a solution might be?"

---

[4] Simon, Cathy Allen. "How to Encourage Higher Order Thinking." Readwritethink.org. National Council of Teachers of English. Web. 19 Dec. 2014. <http://www.readwritethink.org/parent-afterschool-resources/tips-howtos/encourage-higher-order-thinking-30624.html>.

"Why did you decide to choose _____ over _____?"

Try asking children and teens these questions at home and in a variety of educational and non-educational settings. Rather than just having a conversation, you can also ask your child to respond to these questions in writing. Be prepared to respond to your child's answers with even more thought-provoking questions to continue to encourage higher levels of thinking, also opening up the lines of communication between parent and child.

FAMILY MISSION STATEMENT

Contrary to mainstream society, it is fine, almost necessary, for you to decide what you want for your child's future, the type of person you want them to be (leader, healer, warrior, etc.), and exactly what you would like them to achieve. The individualistic concept of "allowing them to be whoever and whatever they want to be" is seriously flawed. Children do not have the experiences or intellectual maturity to decide what they can or cannot do, should and should not do, or who they should and shouldn't be. It takes parents to help shape their concept of the world and their role within it.

The advantage of having a mission statement is that it sets the tone for your child's life. The popular definition of mission statement is a formal summary of the aims and values of a company, organization, or individual. The purpose of a mission statement is to make sure that everyone involved has a common goal, which they base all of their decisions upon. A family mission statement will give the family the opportunity to think about and develop their mission and vision for their family. Everyone blessed with breath has a purpose. Just like every individual, every family should identify their purpose.

In many cultures, families consciously identify and articulate their purpose within the family and the community. For instance, I once had a conversation with a young lady from Nigeria. She was the nurse for my father when he had a serious surgery. To make small talk I asked her where she was from after noticing a strong accent. She said that she was from Nigeria and came here specifically to attend medical school. She went on to tell me that her father told her when she was very young that she would be going to school to become a doctor like her brother, and her sisters were respectively going to become an attorney and a teacher. The plan was that they would get their education and return to serve the community. She

14

explained that everyone in her family had occupations that would contribute to society/their community. This strategic move by her father to establish a mission and goals for his family not only guaranteed that his children would be able to take care of themselves and their families financially, but also guaranteed that they would be able to contribute to their community.

By consciously creating your mission and identifying your goals as a family you establish a foundation for the entire family to base their decisions. When you have identified your mission it controls your desires, your decisions, and affects your attitude. Whenever conflicts arise, or big decisions are being made, the family can refer back to their mission statement to keep them motivated and on track. Below you will find the steps to creating and using your mission statement. Remember this is something the family should do together and revisit often.

Steps to Creating and Using your Family Mission Statement

Step #1 - Engage the whole family.

This is an activity for the entire family, young and elder. Start the meeting by asking the children if they have ever heard of a mission statement and allow them to share what they already know. The more your children feel a part of the process, the more likely they will be to embrace it. Discuss in detail what a mission statement is, why you are establishing one for your family, and the benefits you expect it will bring your family.

Step #2 - Identify specific goals and values based on your family values and principles.

Talk to your children about the purpose for their lives, take time to discuss specific values and goals you have for the family and why those values and goals are important. Explain to them that everyone has an individual purpose, but that each family unit also has a purpose that they should strive for as a unit. Let your children actively participate in the discussion by sharing what they think their purpose and their family purpose is.

Step #3 - Work together to develop the statement.

Be encouraged to be as creative as possible. There is no single format for a family mission statement. It may take the form of a poetic creed, an acronym of your family's last name, or take on some other creative form. The statement can be as long or short as you would like it to be--the easier to remember, the better.

Step#4 - Creatively display and reinforce your family mission statement.

Keep the family mission statement ever present; look for ways to prominently display it in your home. Recite the mission statement daily, at every family meeting, or at least monthly. Also, recognize and celebrate when a family member honors a value or accomplishes a goal that has been identified. The best mission statement in the world won't do anything if you don't revisit and reinforce it. The more you revisit it, the more those key ideas take root.

Step #5 - Evaluate periodically.

Especially if you've never done anything like this before, it may take a while to develop a family mission statement that actually fits your family. Don't feel defeated if your first attempt is not as effective as you desired it to be. Revisit, revise, and stay the course. You may also find that as your children grow and mature that your family mission statement require a bit of modification. Evaluating periodically will allow you to adjust for the different seasons of life your family will go through.

Sample Family Mission Statement

Our mission is to identify our vision, purpose, goals, and aspirations as a family and as individuals in a way that stretches our intellect, enriches our spirit, strengthens our character, and enriches our people, so that we sustain our strength, happiness, confidence, and always stay close.

"A mission statement is not something you write overnight...But fundamentally, your mission statement becomes your constitution, the solid expression of your vision and values. It becomes the criterion by which you measure everything else in your life."
-Stephen Covey

TIME MANAGEMENT

Time management is arguably one of the most important skills a student must have to be successful. This skill is a common problem for students. Many are not taught how to intentionally and independently manage their time. They are awakened by their parents in the morning, a bell tells them when class begins, the teacher tells them when they are dismissed, a bell tells them when lunchtime has come, a bell tells them when they are dismissed from school, and so on. They are not allotted the responsibility to manage their time on their own. Because of this, when it comes time (high school, college and beyond) for the student to manage their time independently, they are not prepared, although they are mercilessly expected to despite their lack of knowledge.

The negative effects that a lack of time management skills has on students are plentiful. I have first hand experience with this deficit as a student myself and with my son. I was (and am still working on it) the biggest procrastinator you could meet. I would wait until the very last minute to begin working on assignments. I would get the work done, but I am sure if I gave myself more time to do the work, I would have gotten even better grades in school. I have noticed this bad habit manifest in my son as well, except he had times where he wouldn't have the time to complete the assignment and ended up receiving horrible grades if not 0's.

Of course, this was absolutely unacceptable. I had to find a solution. I asked other parents, elders, and teachers what strategies I could use to help him develop his time management skills. I tried some of their suggestions and am currently in the process of employing a lot of trial and error to find a solution that works. What I have realized is that time management is not perfected overnight and is something we have to consistently work towards mastering and it involved reevaluating much of our everyday lifestyle.

Below I have provided some of the strategies that helped my son and me develop better time management skills. Do not hesitate to do your own research and look for more strategies. The most important thing for you to remember is that change will not happen overnight. You will become frustrated and it will sometimes seem that your child is just not getting it or even want to get it, but be patient. Don't give up. Improvement will happen and when you see the improvement, even the smallest sign, be sure that you recognize them and celebrate with your child. Small victories lead to big victories.

Strategies to Develop Time Management Skills:

Use Chores to Reinforce Time Management

Create a chart for your child to be hung on their wall and call it "Keepin' it Clean." Use words or images (depending on the age) to illustrate the tasks he/she needs to complete to maintain their room, bathroom, and other rooms in the house. Be sure to include the time frame or amount of time each task should take. This teaches your child how to efficiently finish a set of tasks on his/her own in a timely manner.

Minimize Time Drainers

Television and electronics (tablets, smart phones, game boxes, computers, etc.) are some of the biggest time drainers for children (adults too). Decide with your child how many hours of television/electronics they'll watch/engage with during the week. This should coincide with their daily task schedule. Depending on their homework and chore workload, their time with these extra curricular activities may be very minimal. Some people may say that the child need time to "just chill". I agree, but only IF they complete their task list. If they really desire to have time to watch television or play their games, they will figure out how to complete their tasks in a timely manner.

Time Mapping

This is an especially good exercise for older children (7 to 12 years old) learning to manage their own after-school time. Have your child create a chart that displays all of their responsibilities, be it completing their homework at 5:30 p.m. or doing their chores at 7:30 p.m. Then have them check off each task when they're done. This teaches personal organizational skills and learning to watch the clock.

Example:

Kayla's Time Map

5:30 pm - 6:30 pm	Homework
6:30 pm - 7:30 pm	Chores
7:30 pm - 8:30 pm	Dinner
8:30 pm - 9:00 pm	Prepare for the next day
9:00 pm - 9:30 pm	Reading
9:30 pm	Bedtime

Homework Helper

Have your child make a homework chart and list assignments with due dates for Monday through Friday. This can be in an agenda that carry with them everyday or a chart on the fridge that they have to fill in at the start of each week. After they have finished each assignment, they can put a completion check mark next to it. This teaches children how to keep tabs of their assignments and make sure that they are done in a timely manner. Be careful not to allow them to wait until the very last minute to complete the assignments. This may cause the student to develop the terrible habit of procrastination.

CREATING A LEARNING ENVIRONMENT
CONTROLLING FREQUENCIES

I often take a moment to reflect on the great achievement of my Afrikan ancestors. I think about the pyramids, the temples, the advanced science, technology, mathematics, and literacy that they produced, which to date, are being studied and revered. I believe that we are our ancestors so, naturally, I believe that we can achieve the same greatness. However, the reality is, we are not achieving at such levels. It is my belief that we are not doing so because of all of the distractions we have in our lives.

Our ancestors had the privilege to live as one with nature, something I have personally never been able to experience except on vacations. In the times that I have been able to experience this I found myself more mentally and spiritually clear, and able to perform at a higher level. I was able to think well, more deeply, and more creatively. My brainstorming sessions were more effective and my decision-making was more efficient. I could solve problems easily and felt extremely motivated to stay the course with any challenges that may surface. It never failed, every time I found myself in a more natural environment I found myself not wanting to leave. When your brain is functioning at its peak it is a wonder the things that you can accomplish.

Considering my state of clearer thought in a more natural environment, I began to wonder how much more successful I would be at rearing a child with a sound mind and spirit if I consciously and strategically controlled his environment. How much clearer could he think and how much more would we be able to accomplish if I strategically decreased distractions in our everyday lives? I figured it was worth a try. The main thing I worked to control were the frequencies he was exposed to. This included television, radio, music, video games and the Internet.

Words, music, sounds, our consciousness, our body (indeed the entire universe) is nothing more than vibrations of energy. The rate this energy vibrates is called the frequency. Rocks, emotions, people and even planets differ from each other, and everything else, because of their unique vibrational frequency[5]. Therefore by 'tuning' your brain to certain frequencies makes it is possible to experience different states of consciousness, as well as, stimulating certain brain functions such as creativity or mood enhancement. Consciousness is the state or quality of awareness, or, of being aware of an external object or something within oneself. It has been defined as: sentience, awareness, subjectivity, the ability to experience or to feel, wakefulness, having a sense of selfhood, and the executive control system of the mind[6].

Aside from being absolute time drainers, television, radio, and the Internet are all full of propaganda and have been found to be an effective way to mind control. If the goal is to educate and rear your children with certain values and morals, you must be aware of the impact various forms of mass media has on your mental status, desires and spirit. There was a time where I found myself enthralled in television programming for hours, and spending even more time either thinking about it or talking about it. I even found myself subconsciously basing some of my decisions about reality off of things that were clearly not a reality.

Much of my research in graduate school showed that television is strategically used by the "powers at be" to control the reality of the masses. Your actions reflect what you perceive as your reality. Much of what's offered in media is not only negative, perverted, and unrealistic, but also destructive. It has the power to construct

---

[5] "How Music and Frequencies Affect Our Body and Brain." Mind Power MP3.com. Web. 10 Dec. 2014. <http://www.mindpowermp3.com/Frequencies-music-and-transformation-How-our-audios-work.html>.
[6] "Consciousness." Wikipedia. Wikimedia Foundation. Web. 5 Oct. 2014. <http://en.wikipedia.org/wiki/Consciousness>.

perceptions, understanding about life, goals and aspirations, and ultimately an individual's actions and reactions. This is even truer for children. I find nothing is safe for children to watch or listen to these days. Even the cartoons are laced with violence, sexual innuendos, and capitalistic propaganda.

There was a point when I came to the realization that the frequencies around me were not only negatively affecting me but my child as well. I felt like my son and I should have been spending much more time together. I should have been taking the opportunity to talk to him and allow him to talk to me about things that was on his mind, which is pivotal in the shaping of a child's understanding of the world around them. We spent a lot of time apart, him in one room and me in the other, because what I was watching was not appropriate for him to watch (not realizing that although he wasn't in the room he could hear it and certainly saw what I was watch one way or another, children are pretty clever). Instead of spending time helping him organize his room, looking over his homework or helping him engage in self-study, I was watching television or surfing the Internet. I had convinced myself that it was okay to have some "me time". Everyone deserved some time to just relax and unplug from the world. Although this may be true, the fact still remains that if you have a child, you must consider their well being in everything that you do.

Eventually I began to notice how the frequencies around us were negatively impacting him and his behavior. He began to speak and act very playful and foolish like the cartoons he was watching on television. I found that he would not exude much effort to think deeply about hardly anything. My son began to ask me questions about things that I felt he shouldn't even know about, things that he heard or saw on TV.

Understanding that I was ultimately responsible for controlling his environment and developing a sound minded, well-rounded, mentally, physically, and spiritually healthy individual, I knew I had to begin to take my job of censorship more seriously. I got rid of the television, censored the things that he watched and listened to on the Internet, and took control of the words, sounds, and images that he was being exposed to. If it was not positive or did not contribute to our intellectual development, I did not allow it into our spaces (home or car). I found music that was more empowering and supported our ideology. I found videos online, ones that would be entertaining to him and those that I liked, that supported our morals, values, principles, and ideology and that is what we would watch on the television when we had the time to. I sought out and found music, mostly Hip-Hop, that was dope but also appropriate. Every decision I made was based on the behaviors and aspirations I desired for myself and for my child.

Our lives completely changed once I got rid of cable and I began to become more conscious about:

- what he was exposed to on the internet
- the books he read
- the images around the house (I printed and purchased pictures/posters of images of Afrikan influence, people, and places, purchased a red black and green flag, a character creed for his room, etc.)
- the video games I allowed him to play (there are not many that I approve of)
- the music he and I listened to (I searched high and low and found, what I call liberation music, for us to listen to)
- the radio stations I played in the car (there are not many I approve of)
- the language I use around him (this includes the language I use and don't use, I try to use thought provoking vocabulary at all times and I make a point to make sure he knows what the words I use mean), and we began to have structured dialog about the frequencies around him.

I made it a point to teach him what frequencies are and their effects on his perceptions and reality. We now analyze movies and songs together making a point to identify negative (low) and positive (high) frequencies. This teaches him how to decipher messages on his own, which is important because at some point I know he will be exposed to things that I don't agree with and he will have to make sound decisions on his own.

As you adapt your parenting styles to counter the negative influences your family is exposed to daily, learn from my personal experience rearing my son. Below I have provided a list of the top three (3) things to consider as you progress and evolve:

Key Points to Remember - Frequency (Words, Sounds, and Images)

Words

1. Be conscious of the language being used around your child. This includes the language that you are using while on the phone, or talking to your friends when they are around. This also includes the vocabulary you choose to use when speaking to your child. Do not think you must "dumb down" your vocabulary for your child to understand you. Make them comfortable with letting you know when they don't understand you then teach them what the words mean. This will help build their vocabulary. Also, be conscious of the books your child is reading, especially your higher-level readers. Do a little research if you are unfamiliar with the title or author, you never know what they may be exposed to while engulfed in what you perceive to be a good story.

Sounds

2. Be conscious of the television and radio programming that you are tuning into in your home (and car). If you choose to keep cable, look for programming that does not conflict with the morals and values you teach. There is also good radio programming out there. It will take a little (or a lot) of effort to find them, but is well worth it.

Images

3. Be conscious of the images your child is being exposed to. Try to expose them to as many images that represent your family values, morals, standards, and expectations. For instance, if you value education and the love of your culture, purchase posters with quotes and imagery that encourages it and hang them in your child's room and around the house. You can even find house décor that has meaning.

THEIR FOOD IS THEIR FUEL

Children with unhealthy eating habits often exhibit a failure to thrive. Childhood is a time of critical growth in which proper nutrition is absolutely essential. Children who have poor diets -- whether because of a lack of food or because of patterns of eating that lead to inadequate intake of nutrients needed for healthy development -- are prone to substantial short-term and long-term health impacts and diseases. Youth plagued by prolonged poor nutrition are at greater risk for obesity, mental and emotional health problems, and a failure to thrive academically.

As a teacher, the biggest impact on the emotional and mental health of my students I witnessed was their diet. According to the Children's Defense Fund, "children who do not have access to proper nutrition are much more likely to suffer from psychological disorders, such as anxiety or learning disabilities". These children are also significantly more likely to require mental health counseling. Poor nutrition negatively impacts a child's ability to develop properly and adapt normally to certain situations.

A study in the "Indian Journal of Psychiatry" in 2008, noted a link between iron deficiency and hyperactivity disorders in children. Iodine deficiency has also been linked to some developmental impairment. Certain nutritional habits that children may be prone to, such as skipping meals or overindulging in sugary foods, have also been linked to depression. Additionally, these mental and emotional health problems in children are often accompanied by obesity and low self-esteem, which may be the result of poor nutrition. [7]

---

[7] Fleck, Alissa. "Children With Poor Nutrition." Healthy Eating. SFGate.com. Web. 26 Oct. 2014. <http://healthyeating.sfgate.com/children-poor-nutrition-6555.html>.

Across the nation, black children are being diagnosed (and many times mis-diagnosed) with behavioral and learning disabilities, and my belief is that an unhealthy diet is the culprit.

During my first year teaching I had 17 students, about half of which were either diagnosed with Attention Deficit Hyperactivity Disorder (ADHD) or in process of being diagnosed. Anyone who familiar with this disorder knows that dealing with seven (7) students, who displayed most, if not all of the symptoms, was pretty difficult to do. The hardest part was dealing with the violent, aggressive, and defiant behaviors while still having to love them throughout the process. Much of the students' disruptive behavior was simply that they did not want to sit still.

However, there was one student in particular who was extremely agitated at all times and yearned for attention. He would walk around the classroom destroying shelves, hitting other students, yelling out of turn during whole group discussions, and exhibited other outlandish behaviors. The most memorable moment of his classroom antics was when he threw a chair at me, inches from landing a blow to my head. His behavior caused chaos in my classroom. I knew in order for me to get my classroom under control, I had to learn more about this "disorder" and try to find effective strategies, besides medicines, that would alleviate the symptoms. Several of my students were on medication for the "disorder", but I hated it. The meds would "zombie them out" and the students suffered side effects that were not only counterproductive but down right heartbreaking. I witnessed them experience mood swings, itchiness, dry mouth, nervousness, headache, anxiety, and even tremors. Medication was not the answer.

I began to extensively research ways to help my students deal with their diagnosed conditions. One of the most consistent finding was the importance of the child's diet, in general, and specifically if they show signs of being ADHD, which by the way according to the symptoms, almost everyone can say they experience. I personally believe the disorder is a made up name to rationalize and mask the affects of poor diet, lack of rest, over stimulation, and stress-- you know, the American way of life, but that's another book. What

27

amazed me was the fact that most, if not all, of the foods I observed my students eating were "foods to avoid". What concerned me even more was the fact that many of these foods and drinks were served for school breakfast and lunch, which the majority of my student ate daily. The school served over 90% of free and reduced lunch, meaning these meals (for the most part) were the only meals the parents could afford to give their children and they were very grateful. So this brought me to the dilemma of, how do I help influence the diet of my students knowing the finances of their parents present a barrier to healthier options? My intention of helping would translate into, "Stay away from the only food that you can afford". What were they suppose to do, starve?

Nutrition Makes a Difference

I eventually began to send home literature and hold workshops that emphasized the fact that nutrition and hydration are part of a foundation for healthy learners. Parents making healthy choices and teaching their children how to make healthier choices is an essential part of their education and well-being. One of the biggest issues Afrikan communities are facing right now in America and across the diaspora is the lack of knowledge about, and access to nutritionally rich healthy foods. Much of this is because of systematic racism and oppression affecting the health education received, financial capability to afford healthier foods, and access to housing that is accessible to healthier food options. In the past 10 years I have personally experienced living in several areas where fast food and grocery stores with tiny fresh organic sections were the only options I had within 30 miles, and this is historically found in predominantly Afrikan areas and very much so intentional. However, there are things that we can do to take control of our eating lifestyles that we frankly are not buckling down and doing.

A lot of the decisions made regarding our diets are not in efforts to heal and fuel our bodies but are made for convenience and pleasure. Don't get me wrong, I understand the fact that many of us inherited horrible eating habits and diets. It's all we know. Our grandparents and parents did the best that they could. With this being the age of information however, it is important for us to become educated and acknowledge the damage our diets are making on our children and families, and begin to teach the present and future generations better eating habits and the diets of our ancestors, and we must do this by example. Our ancestors lived off of the land, not out of a box, bag, or bottles. For their optimal health (mental, physical, and spiritual) children must be fed nutritionally rich foods, vitamins, and herbs, and must stay away from foods and drinks that are not. It's hard and it takes effort and sacrifice, but it is detrimental to not only the health of our children but also the health of our community.

I personally make an effort to follow the Kemetic way of eating. This is the way that our ancestors ate. Our ancestors many times lived to surpass 100 years of age. Their diet played a significant role in this phenomenon. I figured who better to learn from and follow the ways of than those who proved to thrive. The Kemetic Diet is based on the teachings and lifestyle of the Ancient Africans who lived in Kemet (today referred to as Ancient Egypt). Kemetic eating is basically the concept of eating only when you are hungry and only eating food that nourish and heal your body. Kemetic eaters believe that consuming processed foods, sugar, and salt leads to health problems and should be eliminated from the diet completely.

Following the Kemetic Diet has proven to be a way to improve my son's and my mental, physician and spiritual health through proper food for the mind, body and soul. It even proves to be a way to heal if disease comes. Like everything else, our ancestors were very strategic in the way they ate. They understood and listened to their bodies. Their meals were not for mere pleasure like they are for many of us today. Their meals were very much so purposeful.

We should get back to eating this way. Nature provides the foods and herbs our bodies need to thrive and heal. There are things that help every system in your body thrive, from the immune system to the nervous (brain) system. These are the foods and herbs that we should be ingesting. This is how we can get back to thriving and not just surviving, and many times suffering at the hands of our diet.

Below I have provided a list of Do's and Don'ts as well as tips that may help you work your way towards or continue an optimally healthy productive diet and lifestyle.

Do's

- Offer several fruit and vegetable options every day. Don't feel bad if you can't always find fresh fruits and vegetables. Frozen and canned fruits and vegetables are good options, too. If you choose canned fruits, look for those that are canned in their own juices or light syrup as opposed to heavy syrup.

- Provide healthy sources of protein. As a vegan and one who follow the Kemetic Diet I can't in good conscious encourage you to eat meat, what most people think of when looking for protein. You don't need to eat meat or cheese to get enough protein. Peas, pea hummus quinoa, nut and nut butter, beans, chickpeas, broccoli, non-dairy meats, lentils, and sprouted-grain bread all provide just as much, if not more, protein than meat.

- Serve whole-grain breads and cereals

- Broil, grill or steam foods instead of frying them

- Limit fast food, carry-out and junk food. When eating at fast-food or other restaurants, choose the healthiest options from the menu, such as fruit instead of French fries and grilled chicken with mustard instead of a hamburger with cheese and a creamy sauce. Choose salads with low-fat dressings over fried foods. Order thin-crust instead of deep-dish pizza and small instead of a medium or a medium instead of a large.

- Encourage your child to drink plenty of water instead of sugar-added drinks such as fruit juice, sugar-sweetened fruit drinks, regular-calorie soft drinks, sports drinks, energy drinks, sweetened or flavored milk or sweetened iced tea.

- Read labels. The Nutrition Facts label on packaged foods lists a variety of useful information, including the serving size, calories and nutrients per serving, and more.

- When reading labels, keep in mind that the ingredients are typically listed in order of predominance. So if, for example, you were reading a cereal label, it would be best for the first ingredient to be a grain, not fructose or high fructose corn syrup or sucrose/sugar.

- Instead of purchasing numerous full meals and drinks, share with your child(ren). You would be surprised at how many servings are in one meal from a restaurant.

- Include a healthy, nutrient rich, breakfast in the daily line-up. Breakfast is very important to give your child the energy he or she needs to fuel learning. Avoid feeding your child(ren) sugar-filled breakfast foods and other breakfast foods that lack nutritional value. NO FAST FOOD FOR BREAKFAST.

- Avoid fried snacks. Opt for fruit or nuts. If fruit and nuts are unavailable, opt for baked chips and pretzels or unbuttered popcorn instead of fried snacks.

- Don't insist that your child "clean the plate." You are on task to ensure your child has healthy food options in the house, but let your child determine how much to eat. Don't push food.

- Avoid using desserts or treats as rewards or comfort. This may make your child value those foods more than nutritious options.

- Be a good role model for your child. Make sure that you are making healthy food choices and incorporating exercise into your life.

- Get the whole family involved in eating a healthier diet. Teach them how to make healthy decisions and reward them when they do.

- Eat meals and snacks together as a family as often as possible. Eat at the table, not in front of the television or in separate rooms.

- Encourage your child to eat slowly and to stop eating when he or she starts to feel full.

Don'ts

- **Processed Foods** - this includes "foods" in a box or bag. Many of the food additives that are perfectly legal to use in US foods are banned in other countries. When foods are processed, not only are valuable nutrients lost and fibers removed, but also the textures and natural variation and flavors are also lost. After processing, what's left behind is a bland, uninteresting "pseudo-food" that most people wouldn't want to eat. So at this point, food manufacturers must add back in the nutrients, flavor, color and texture to processed foods in order to make them palatable, and this is why they become loaded with dangerous food additives, many linked to learning and behavior disorders.

- **Sugary Food and Drinks** - Research suggests that there are many negative effects associated with children consuming diets heavy in refined sugars, including obesity, hyperactivity and malnutrition. Sugars, however, come in many forms. Typically, refined sugar refers to white sugar, but it can also refer to several types of other added sugars, which may make sugars on a food label difficult to identify. Sugar-sweetened beverages are one of the major culprits in the obesity epidemic, but sodas have also been connected to behavioral problems among teens. That link apparently extends to young children as well. Among children five (5) years old, according to the latest research[8], those drinking more sugar-sweetened sodas showed increased aggression, withdrawal and difficulty paying attention than those drinking fewer or none of the beverages.

[8]Sifferlin, Alexandra. "Soda Contributes to Behavior Problems Among Young Children." Time - Soda Contributes to Behavior Problems Among Young Children. Time, 16 Aug. 2013. Web. 16 Nov. 2014.

- **Soy Products**[9] - AVOID. In order to comply with new US Government standards, soy products are now being used to replace whole, nutritious foods in school lunches. Due to the decreased fat content of soy, it is touted as a healthful alternative to the meat and dairy of yesterday's hot meal. Nothing could be further from the truth. Soy added to your child's hot lunch depletes the necessary nutrients needed for healthy growth and has been linked to learning disabilities. Do your children a favor and send them to school with a healthy, home-packed meal.

More Tips:

- Subscribe to this rule of thumb - If there are more than five (5) ingredients in it, it's not good for you
- Shop the perimeter of the store where you will find less processed foods
- Try not to shop when hungry. People tend to make poorer decisions when their bellies are talking.
- Cook more. It's always better when you can control the ingredients.
- If you do go out to eat, stay away from fried and sugary foods. Also, use this time to teach your children how to choose healthier items from the menu.
- Teach children how to choose the healthiest foods from the menu that is available
- Be aware of your school's Wellness Policy and either contribute to, or obtain support for, change in your classroom/school
- Push your child's school to incorporate nutrition education into various areas of their curriculum

---

[9]"The Dirty Little Secret Hidden in Some Health Foods - Soy Products." Mercola.com. Mercola, 8 Dec. 2011. Web. 16 Feb. 2015.
<http://articles.mercola.com/sites/articles/archive/2011/12/08/the-dirty-little-secret-hidden-in-much-of-your-health-food.aspx>.

READING IS FUNDAMENTAL

What's the most important trait you'd like to develop in your child? If you're like most parents, intelligence is probably at the top of your list. All parents desire intelligent, well-rounded children, which is why we concern ourselves with choosing the right schools and making sure teachers are meeting or exceeding expectations. But you should be reminded that ultimately, as a parent, you have the power to boost your children's learning potential simply by making reading an integral part of their lives.

Reading truly is fundamental. I have found that if a student struggles with reading they most likely will struggle with most of the other content areas. In order to ensure your child is able to expand their knowledge in a subject area, they will need to master the skill of reading with comprehension. However, do not allow your child's skill development to be limited to the classroom. There are many strategies parents can implement at home to ensure their child excels in their reading and comprehension skills. As parents, you should begin teaching reading skills as soon as possible.

I began to teach my son how to read around 2 years old. As a professional early childhood education teacher, I learned how to teach children how to read in my teacher-training program. However, I learned some of the most effective strategies during my self-study. I researched how to teach children how to read as early as one years old and I found plenty of programs that claimed to teach children how to read in a short amount of time, and how to teach them to read on an advanced level. To my surprise, there was no secret formula. Patience, diligence, and consistency were key.

If you truly want your child(ren) to be successful at teaching your child how to read, you must be willing to research various strategies, ask their teacher for tips, look for books, search the web, ask other parents, be willing to at least try the strategies you find, and continue to do so until you find strategies that work for your child. Once you find the strategies that work, you must be consistent (give it at least 5 weeks before you "give up"). Also, it is beneficial to keep record of the various strategies you try with your child(ren). Document how effective or ineffective you find each to be, and why. This will help you accurately track the effectiveness of the strategies. There are bound to be times when you feel like you are just spinning wheels to no avail when in actuality you may just be close to a breakthrough.

I once had a student whose parents enrolled him into my homeschool program mainly because the school system was trying to not only place him in special education but was also advising that he be placed in a "special school" where there were no "regular classrooms". His mother took one visit to the "special school", describing it as a child's prison, and withdrew him from the school district and brought him to me. With tears in her eyes she proclaimed, "I just want my baby to learn. I know he's smart. I know he can get it. He just needs some time."

His mother was right, he needed time but as many know, time is a luxury in schools today. Her student was in the third grade reading on a pre-K level. He could barely identify the alphabet and possessed little to no literacy skills. I suggested that his parents allow me to focus on reading for most of the year including the other content areas if time allotted. I knew that once you get a child reading with comprehension you can easily teach them the content area skills needed. His parents complied and for much of the school year we focused on getting him reading on his grade level.

Every moment of the day was used as a teachable moment. I posted words around the house (like in the movie *The Color Purple*), had him read street signs as we drove around, and had him practicing every hour on the hour. I tried almost everything to ensure his reading skills improved. At first, it was difficult for both of us as we battled low confidence and the embarrassment he suffered. To make matters even more challenging, he was bigger and taller than most of the students. Nonetheless, we stayed the course and pushed through. His victory was glorious, and the value of his achievement is beyond words. His enthusiasm to learn increased tremendously and his confidence soared through the roof. This student began to ask to read during class, something he had never dared to do in the past and an accomplishment of which he was clearly proud. As rewarding as this process was, parents please remember that these results were not produced overnight and are unsustainable if not nurtured consistently.

Every child learns differently so I'm always careful not to give the impression that there is some secret formula or curriculum that will produce the same results for every child. There are skills that all students must learn at some point, but there are many ways that these skills can be taught. The key is to figure out your child's most effective learning style and what type of instructional strategies they enjoy the most. The more they enjoy the instruction the more engaged they will be and the more they will learn.

Parents have to muster up the determination to make the necessary effort to do the research, implement their selected strategies, be persistent, and never give up. However, do not limit your efforts and resources to your household, reach out to your extended family and get everyone in your child's life involved. The proverb still reigns true, "It takes a village to raise a child." Inform everyone involved in your child's life of the strategies you are trying, and ask them to implement the same practices, at least during the time they interact with your child. No amount of effort is too great. The child will appreciate and benefit from the group effort.

Below I have provided a list of strategies that worked for me as I worked with students on improving reading comprehension. Try them for yourself and see if any work for you and your child. If they prove to be ineffective, take the time to research other strategies and/or programs that may work for you. Trust me, you will be forever grateful for a literate child, and the earlier they master reading, the better.

Tips To Help Teach Your Child To Read[10]:

1. Read to your child

Teaching your child to read is truly a process that begins at infancy. Begin reading with your newborn within days of welcoming them home. This can serve as a special bonding time for the two of you, and instills in them a love for books and reading.

Enjoyment while reading is one of the single greatest predictors of potential academic success in school-age children. If children don't learn from an early age to enjoy reading, it will most likely hinder their ability to achieve in the future. How much you read to your child is completely up to you and your family, but aim to read at least 20-minutes each day.

Here are a few suggestions for the types of books to read to your child at different stages of development, but by all means, read whatever your child responds to and enjoys!

- **Birth - 1 Year**: Lullabies, Board Books (with real pictures), Cloth Books (with various textures), Song Books
- **1 Year - 3 Years**: Rhyming Books, Song Books, Short-Story Board Books
- **3 Years - 5 Years**: Alphabet Books, Song Books, Picture Books, Rhyming Books, Folktales & Fables

2. Ask questions

Asking questions while reading to your child is not only great for encouraging your child to interact with the book, but it is also extremely effective in developing their ability to comprehend what they are reading. If our main objective of "reading" is getting our child to "sound out" words, we have missed the purpose entirely. Even children who can decode words and "read" with great fluency still might not be able to understand what they are reading. If a child

---

[10] "10 Steps to Teaching Your Child to Read - I Can Teach My Child!" I Can Teach My Child. 24 Feb. 2012. Web. 7 Jan. 2015. <http://www.icanteachmychild.com/10-steps-to-teaching-your-child-to-read/>.

can't comprehend what he is reading, beyond mastering phonetics, there really is no point to reading at all.

While your child is a baby, ask him/her questions such as, "Do you see the cat?" while pointing at the picture of the cat. This will not only develop their vocabulary, it will also encourage them to interact with the book that they are reading. As they get older, ask them to point to things in the book and expand on what they see. For example, when reading a book with animals as the subject and your child points to various animals, mimic the noises of the animals they see to make learning exciting and fun. Not only will this improve the practicality of reading, as they are able to make the connection to not only the word and the picture, but to the animal's function/sounds.

Once your child is two (2) or three (3) years of age, begin asking questions before, during, and after reading the book. This will help develop their ability to predict, infer, connect and summarize texts in the future. Show your child the cover of the book and ask them what they think it's going to be about (predicting). While reading, ask them what they think is going to happen or why they think a character made a particular choice (inferring). If a character is depicting a strong emotion, identify that emotion and ask your child if they have ever felt that way (connecting). At the end of the book, ask if their prediction(s) came true. After reading the story, ask them to tell you what they remembered happening in the book (summarizing). Modifying each of these techniques to meet the developmental stage of your child is a great way to promote and increase reading comprehension.

3. Be a good (reading) example

Even if your child is fascinated with books at an early age, their fascination can quickly dwindle if they do not see reading modeled in their home. If you are not an avid reader yourself, make a conscious effort to let your children see you reading for at least a few minutes each day. Read a magazine, a cookbook, a novel, or inspirational reading. Show your child that reading is something that even adults need to do.

As parents, we can sometimes get wrapped up with what exactly our children should be doing to be successful, often forgetting that children learn by example.

4. Identify letters/words in natural settings

In technical terms, this process is called "environmental print" and includes all of the printed text we are surrounded by–fast food signs, labels, traffic signs, clothing, magazines, etc.

Often times, we want to force our children to learn the alphabet by a certain age. We buy flashcards or DVDs claiming to teach our children their letters. We drill our 2-year old over and over for minutes on end. All of these strategies are good, but allow your child to be a child, and take advantage of the "teachable moments" as they come along. Children's minds are like sponges and are certainly capable of memorizing the alphabet from drilling, but that's not the most effective method that will produce the best long-term results.

Your child will be curious about the print he sees around him and will ask questions. This is your chance to teach them a practical application that actually has meaning and significance to your child. I am not implying that learning the alphabet isn't important, but the method you choose to teach is even more important. Always keep in mind that your ultimate goal is to develop a lifelong learner who loves to read, not a child who has simply memorized without any significance.

THE IMPORTANCE OF DIALOGUE

di·a·logue
'dīəˌläg,'dīəˌlôg/
noun

1. a discussion between two or more people or groups, especially one directed toward exploration of a particular subject or resolution of a problem" the U.S. would enter into a direct **dialogue with** Vietnam"

2. take part in a conversation or discussion to resolve a problem. "He stated that he wasn't going to **dialogue with** the guerrillas"
                                                                  -Google Definition

It is extremely important for parents to have continued dialogue with their children. Children want to know everything, and they observe and soak up everything around them. My son asks me questions every 5 minutes on the dot it seems. "Mama, Mama, Mama"; there are times when I have to tell him that Mama needs a break, but most of the time I consciously make sure that I answer all of his questions. Even if I don't know the answers, I make it a point to make the effort to find the answer. There is always an advantage when parents are able to contribute to their child's conceptualization of the world and they're role in it. This develops their worldview.

Earlier we discussed the importance of asking questions. As important as it is to allow children to ask their questions, it is equally important for parents to ask children questions. Asking questions will help you to keep up with what your child is learning, and their perceptions of their experiences and the world around them. Sometimes you will be surprised what your child has been exposed to. Most children have a world of their own in their heads. They have vivid imaginations. Naturally, as a child, they lack the learned experiences and intellectual development to understand complex concepts and experiences. This is why it is very important for parents to provide a safe environment for children to engage in dialogue where they are allowed to ask questions and gain knowledge and wisdom from responsible adults and elders in their lives. It seems that there is a disconnection between the elders and the children in our community, and I believe that this is because of the lack of dialogue amongst the youth, family members, and the community. This has proven to be detrimental to our children. They find themselves having to comprehend the world on their own. Without the guidance of parents and elders, children typically look to mass media, music, and television to gain an understanding of their experiences and curiosities, leaving them with a false sense of reality.

When you send your child to school, you are entrusting another human being with their own experiences, biases, life principles, objectives and opinions to teach your child. Considering this, it is safe to say that you cannot be absolutely sure that they are being taught accurate facts, the same morals and values as you are upholding, or that the instructors have your child's best interest at heart.

In my experience I have heard teachers teaching inaccurate content and displaying behaviors that contradicts some of the most common morals and values. During my son's 3rd grade year, the teacher planned to teach a unit on popular winter holidays, Kwanzaa being one of them. She sent an email out asking for parents to send in red, green, and white ribbon to be used for the Kwanzaa project that they were doing. I immediately "replied all" letting her know that the ribbon should be red, black, and green which is common knowledge for those who celebrate Kwanzaa.

The symbolism of the candles' colors is a major component of the holiday and its meaning. Her lack of knowledge wasn't what raised a red flag for me; it was her lack of research on a topic of which she clearly was unfamiliar. This prompted me to question her overall instruction in the classroom. I asked her for a copy of the lesson plan (which is every parent's right) and I was floored with the inaccuracies I found. Of course the teacher in me drafted another lesson plan that possessed the correct information about Kwanzaa and requested that she refrain from teaching the other lesson. I emailed her, highlighting the inaccuracies within the lesson plan, and attached supporting documentation. I also sent a carbon copy of the email to the instructional coach and school administration to be sure they were aware of the feedback and suggestions provided. As parent's we often receive what teachers tell us without raising any questions. I encourage all parents to take charge and have dialogue with both their children and teachers.

This ordeal led to me being more vigilant when it came to what was being taught in class at his school. From that point on I requested the curriculum map and lesson plans for every unit. The teacher did not like my requests and the administration expressed their opinion that I was being unreasonable, but I did not bend. It was necessary for me to know what my child was being taught as facts. It was clear that I could not trust that his teacher would do sufficient research during her preparation for her lessons.

Admittedly, because I am an experienced educator, doing this was second nature for me and may be too much to ask parents to do. However, I do advise parents to at the very least have a dialogue with your child(ren) daily (or often) about what they are learning in school. This will help you to gauge what the child is being taught at the time and give you the opportunity to add your perspective and correct mis-education if necessary. Also, ask your student about their teacher. Ask them questions about his/her character. Children will tell you everything. Make sure that the teacher is upholding at least the most common ethical moral values and principles (respect, age-appropriate behavior and conversation around the children, appropriate attire, etc.).

It is also important for you to be aware of the things your child is learning from others in the environments they find themselves frequenting. This means their grandparents' home, dad's home (if you are not living in the same home), your friend's home, the after school program, your place of worship, etc. Remember, your child absorbs everything around them, good and bad. It is up to you to do your due diligence making sure your child is around environments and individuals that are conducive to their development mentally, physically, and spiritual. If your child regularly visits their grandparent's home and you know someone in the home frequently watches inappropriate television programming, it is your duty to ask them to refrain from watching it around your child. This is not nitpicking; this is taking your responsibility to rear your child well seriously. Believe it or not, all that your child is exposed to shapes their reality.

The ultimate goal is for your child to feel comfortable talking to you maybe not about every thing, but at least most things. Because parents serve as nurturers and disciplinarians, many times children are not comfortable with coming to you if they feel like you will not like what they will be telling you, or the question that they have. They may feel like (or have been told) they will "get in trouble" if they come to you about it. This is especially true when it comes to "sensitive" or "commonly controversial" yet largely important topics like their realization of their attraction to the opposite sex, sex, religion, and recreational activities like drugs and partying.

During your dialogues be conscious of your body language and their body language. Be careful not to react in a manner that will make them NEVER come to you again. Listen to them without interrupting. Ask questions for clarity if necessary. Think first, then respond. Don't feel like you must respond immediately. If necessary, take some time out to think about how you will respond. Consider how you felt when you had these questions growing up because nothing is new under the sun. You were once your child. Base your response on the morals and values that you are teaching your child and respond reasonably. "You shouldn't be thinking about girls right now" is not a good response to a growing boy. He should be thinking about girls. Be happy that he is. A better response would be to ask him questions like, "Why do you like her? What do you want to do about it? Do you think she likes you?" This will break the ice a bit and certainly may cause some giggles and embarrassment, but it will show the child that you are open about the conversation. Once he answers the questions, discuss your perspective and your expectations of him around the topic.

The most important thing for parents to do when having dialogue with your child is to check your biases based on your experiences at the door. Do not respond through the vein of emotion. It's okay to share your experiences (where appropriate) with your child, but be careful not to project your biases, disdain, disappointments, and or negative emotions around the topic. These are yours to own according to your experiences, not your child's. If men have always hurt you throughout your life, be careful not to teach your daughter to be afraid of men or to hate men. Do the work that you need to do to heal before you begin to have conversations with your daughter about men. You may need to seek council from an elder or another woman who has had healthy relationships with men to gain a more positive perspective before you begin to have those conversations with your daughter. And don't be too proud to allow others in to help you. A mother of one of the young ladies I've worked with over the years expressed her gratitude for our relationship explaining that there were a lot of things that she desired to teach her child but she felt she lacked the adequate knowledge/wisdom or access to resources to do so. As she went down the list of things she saw I was able to address with her child, I was honored to know I was able to serve in her stead.

I'd like to add, as a word of caution, in your effort to build a strong relationship with your child, be cognizant of what they are saying around their children. Even in what we consider to be general conversations about life or praise to others, we project our views and biases. Our children hear us more than we know. This may affect our child's perception and can either encourage or discourage them from discussing their thoughts about the topic with us.

Below you will find a list of tips that will help open and keep open the lines of communication with your child. Continued dialogue with your child will help you to assess their understanding about reality and give you the opportunity to contribute to their understanding.

Tips to help open (and keep open) the lines of communication with your child:

- Consider this genuine relationship building, because that is what you are doing. It is necessary for you to focus on rearing your child, but remember too that you are rearing an able body, responsible, responsive, emotional, reflective, very intelligent individual who will one day become an adult, one that you should hope to have a good relationship with later in your lives.

- Be an approachable parent. Encourage your child to come to you when they need help by reacting in a nonjudgmental way and helping them solve their problems. Your immediate reactions should not be for you to tell them if they are in the right or wrong.

- Find time to spend together. Be involved in something that your child is involved in, even if it is just being a fan at their games. This will give you a common topic to talk about. Families that hardly spend time together have a harder time communicating with each other. Get creative about scheduling family time. For instance, if dinners are taken up with sports games and practices, have breakfasts together, or surprise them with lunch at school when time allots.

- Use the time you have together to connect. For example, don't sit at the dinner table reading emails or scrolling through your social media timelines.

- Ask a mixture of specific and open-ended questions. Listen, using your active listening skills (pay attention, show that you're listening, defer judgment, provide feedback, and respond appropriately). Take a bit of time to think before responding if necessary.

- Be careful not to criticize your child, even when he or she does something wrong. It's the behavior that is wrong or bad, not your child. Rather, give a firm critique of their behavior and discuss possible consequences and solutions.

- Be positive. Talk about what is good in your life, even if it is trivial. Talk about how you manage to keep a positive attitude despite the struggles you face and generously express your gratefulness for the blessings in your life. You'll be modeling a positive attitude to your child.

- Remember to give praise when praise is due. Understand that too much praise is counterproductive, but due praise is necessary to your child's self-esteem development.

- Don't be too proud to admit when you are wrong. Communicating to your child that you have made a mistake builds trust.

CHARACTER DEVELOPMENT

Character is a pattern of behavior, thoughts and feelings based on universal principles, moral strength, and integrity – plus the guts to live by those principles every day[11]. Your life's virtues and the "line you never cross" evidence character. Character is the most valuable thing you have, and nobody can ever take it away. Character in life is what makes people believe in you and is essential both for individual success and for our society to function successfully.

Parents must teach their children that each individual must do his or her part every day by living a life of integrity. Integrity is adhering to a moral code of honesty, courage, strength and truthfulness – being true to your word. When you don't exhibit integrity, other people get hurt. But you hurt yourself even more. When you cheat, your "success" is false. When you break a promise, you are showing that your word is meaningless. When you lie, you deceive others and lose their respect. These examples destroy your reputation and break the trust others have in you.

Relationships are the foundation for success in life. Without a good reputation and trustworthiness, your relationships fail. By breaking your relationships, you break the foundation for success in your life. Parents should make it clear to their children that good character is the most important asset they can have. It takes a lifetime to build a reputation but it can be lost in an instant. Once lost, it is difficult to regain. Reinforce to your student the fact that true character is revealed when no one else is looking. Teach them not to act based on short-term gain, or an easy fix to a problem. They will end up doing the wrong thing. The old saying "you are what you do" is true. Parents must teach their children, failure to consider the long-term consequences of their acts can be disastrous for them and/or the

---

[11] "CITRS » Why Is Character So Important?" CITRS. Web. 19 Nov. 2014.
<http://www.citrs.org/what-is-character/why-is-character-so-important/>.

people around them. By parents studying and focusing on the importance of character children are more prone to be guided by principles, moral strength, and integrity to do the right thing.

As a teacher I've seen what good character development can do for a child's overall emotional, moral, and intellectual health/stability. Students who understand the importance of good character experience higher academic performance and display more productive behaviors. Exceptional character help prepare students to face the many opportunities and adversities life will present them in a manner that is productive for them and their community. Character helps them to navigate the world and play a productive role in shaping their reality and contributing to the reality of those around them.

Today's youth are exposed to an abundance of negative influences, through the media and their peers every day. Additionally, due to their financial obligations in taking care of their family and financial marginalization, parents are spending less time with their children. Children must understand how to handle life's situations many times without the help from parents or other adults around them. Helping to develop their character by instilling a strong set of principles and expectations provide children the necessary tools to make sound decisions.

Religious practices and spiritual systems are often times the foundation of ones character development. Many times parents neglect to do their spiritual studies and practices/rituals alongside their children believing that they may be too young to understand. This should not be the case. It is essential for parents to be clear with their children about their spiritual principles, which are the foundation of their morals and values. When parents explain this, the children feel less like they are merely following rules and have more of an understanding of morals and values as a way of supreme, joyous, fulfilled, righteous living. Additionally, children who are exposed to conversations and literature surrounding spirituality tend to think more critically. They are more thoughtful and tend to possess better decision-making skills. They possess good character.

The 42 Laws of Maat and ancient Afrikan principles are my references for the development of character. In an effort to keep them forever present and a consistent frame of reference, I printed out the principles and 42 Laws and posted them on the walls of our home. We constantly discuss the meaning of them and how they relate to our everyday lives. Additionally, I searched for and found a book that reinforces the principles. We take time daily to read and discuss a passage from the book. At times where character flaws arise, I use the principles and laws to reinforce how and why the behavior is unacceptable and the affect it has on not only his life but also his community.

Below I have listed tips that I have adapted from Helen LeGette's Twenty Strategies to Help Your Children to Develop Good Character[12]. These tips are helpful as you intentionally develop character in children and adults alike. It is important for parents to keep the character development of their child intentional and everlasting. This will prove to be one of the best things you could do for your child. It will minimize unsound decision-making and increase your child's chances for success.

Tips for developing character in your child:

- **Be a role model.** The notion of "Do as I say, not as I do" truly is not effective. It is critically important that those who are attempting to influence children's character in positive ways to "walk the talk."

- **Be clear about your values.** Tell your children where you stand on important issues. Good character is both taught and caught. If we want children to internalize the virtues that we value, we need to teach them what we believe and why. In the daily living of our lives, there are countless opportunities to engage children in moral conversation.

---

[12] LeGette, Helen. "CharacterEd.Net - Twenty Strategies to Help Your Children Develop Good Character." *Twenty Strategies to Help Your Children Develop Good Character.* National Center for Youth Issues or from the Character Development Group. Web. 16 Feb. 2015. <http://charactered.net/parent/parenttwenty.asp>.

- **Show respect for your significant other, your children, and other around you.** Parents who honor each other, who share family responsibilities, and who resolve their differences in peaceful ways reinforces a powerful message about respect. If children consistently experience respect firsthand within their environment, they are more likely to be respectful of others. If they are consistently exposed to uncontrolled aggression and disrespect, they are more likely to behave as such. Simply stated, respect produces respect.

- **Model and teach your children good manners.** Insist that all family members use good manners in the home. It is in the home that thoughtfulness for others has its foundation.

- **Have family meals together without television as often as possible.** Mealtime is an excellent time for parents to talk with and listen to their children and to strengthen family ties. Whether the meal is a home-cooked feast or at a restaurant, the most important ingredient is the sharing time — the time set aside to reinforce a sense of belonging to and being cared about by the family.

- **Plan as many family activities as possible.** Involve your children in the planning. Family activities that seem quite ordinary at the moment are often viewed in retrospect as very special and memorable bits of family history. A dad's "date" with a teenage daughter, a family gathering in the park, or a Sunday excursion for vegan treats can provide a meaningful time for being together and sharing as a family.

- **Don't provide your children access to alcohol or drugs.** Model appropriate behavior regarding alcohol and drugs (prescription and recreational). Despite peer pressure, the anxieties of adolescence, a youthful desire for sophistication, and media messages that glamorize the use of drugs and alcohol, the family is the most powerful influence on whether a young person will become a substance abuser. Nowhere is the parents' personal example more critical than in the area of alcohol and drug use.

- **Plan family service projects or civic activities.** At the heart of good character is your child's understanding that they are a part of a whole. Ubuntu is an African principle that reinforces the concept of "I am because WE are" which is indeed true. In a society where most families live in silos and individualism is prevalent, it is difficult to teach this principle. There are few examples of people behaving in a manner that reinforces it. Nonetheless, numerous opportunities for family service projects where even young children can participate exist in every community. Simple acts like taking food to a sick neighbor, mowing an elderly person's yard, or collecting outgrown clothes and toys for charity help youth learn the joys of assisting others and develop lifelong habits of service that reinforces the Ubuntu principle.

- **Read to your children and keep good literature in the home.** Great teachers have always used stories to teach, motivate, and inspire, and reading together is an important part of passing the moral legacy of our culture from one generation to another. Children's questions and comments about the stories offer parents important insights into their children's thoughts, beliefs, and concerns.

- **Go against the grain of capitalism.** Help them develop an appreciation for non-material rewards. In today's consumerist culture, youth could easily come to believe that image — wearing the "right" clothes, driving the "right" car, etc. — represents the path to success and happiness. Parents can make strong statements about what they value by the ways in which they allocate their own resources and how they allow their children to spend the funds entrusted to them.

- **Establish and discuss the family traditions and their meanings.** Have family celebrations and establish family traditions. Family celebrations and traditions provide a source of identity, strengthen the family bond, offer a sense of comfort and security amongst the family unit, teach and reinforce family values, add to the rhythm and seasonality of life, pass on cultural and spiritual heritage, connect generations, and create lasting memories. Celebrating family traditions not only develop these feelings of attachment to and kinship with others, but they also serve as a special kind of glue that binds us together as universal beings, as family members, and as a people.

- **Capitalize on the "teachable moment."** Use situations to spark family discussions on important issues. Some of the most effective character education can occur in the ongoing, everyday life of the family. As parents and children interact with one another and with others outside the home, there are countless situations that can be used to teach valuable lessons about responsibility, empathy, kindness, and compassion.

- **Assign home responsibilities to all family members.** Even though it is often easier to clear the table, take out the trash, or load the dishwasher ourselves than to wait for a child to do it, we have an obligation to help children learn to balance their own needs and wishes against those of other family members — and ultimately, other members of society.

- **Set clear expectations for your children and hold them accountable for their actions.** Defining reasonable limits and enforcing them appropriately establishes the parents as the moral leaders in the home and provides a sense of security to children and youth. It also lets them know that you care enough about them to want them to be — or to become — people of good character.

- **Keep your children busy in positive activities.** Children and youth have remarkable energy levels, and the challenge is to channel that energy into positive activities such as sports, hobbies, music or other forms of the arts, or youth groups or clubs. Such activities promote accountability, selflessness, caring, and cooperation, and also give children a sense of accomplishment.

- **Learn to say no and mean it.** It is natural for children — especially teenagers — to test the limits and challenge their parents' authority. Despite the child's protests, a parent's most loving act is often to stand firm and prohibit the child's participating in a potentially hurtful activity.

- **Know where your children are, what they are doing, and with whom.** Adults need to communicate in countless ways that we care about children and that we expect the best from them, but also that we take seriously our responsibility to establish standards and to monitor, chaperone, and supervise. Never hesitate to insist on meeting your children's friends and their parents, at every stage of their childhood.

- **Refuse to condone or support unacceptable behavior.** Shielding children and youth from logical consequences of their actions fails to teach them personal responsibility and accountability. It also undermines the fact that all causes have an affect and all actions have consequences. They should never be under the impression that they are somehow exempt from the consequences of their actions.

- **Know what television programming, Internet entertainment, and movies your children are watching.** While there are some very fine materials available, a proliferation of pornographic and disturbing information is easily accessible to our youth. By word and example, teach your children responsible viewing habits. If you learn that your child has viewed something objectionable, candidly share your feelings and discuss why the material goes against your family's values and expectations.

- **Remember that you are the adult.** Children don't need another buddy, but they desperately need a parent who cares enough to set and enforce appropriate limits for their behavior. Sometimes being able to say, "My dad won't let me" provides a convenient escape for a youth who really didn't want to participate in a questionable activity.

STAYING INVOLVED AND INFORMED

It is important for parents to understand that the responsibility of education is not solely on the schools and teachers. A child's intellectual development is first the parent's responsibility. The school and teachers should be seen as a support system to their child's development. This is not the case in today's society.

Schooling is very much seen as the sole responsibility of the educational institution. As a matter of fact, society makes it seem as though the parent is the last person who is skilled enough to educate their children, so much so that parents barely feel as if they have any control, power, or influence when it comes to the education of their children, but this is far from true. This way of thinking has been detrimental, taking a very important aspect of child development out of the hands of the parents who have the sole responsibility of rearing them.

Consider how many hours a child of working parents actually spends under the tutelage of their parents. Who do they really spend the most time with? The reality is students spend the majority of their time in school. The average American student spends 220 out of 365 days in school[14]. Considering this fact, it is extremely important for parents to stay involved and informed as to what is going on in their child's school as much as they can. Any time that they can spare should be spent becoming involved and informed.

---

[14] Hull, Jim, and Mandy Newport. "Time in School: How Does the U.S. Compare?" Time in School: How Does the U.S. Compare? 1 Dec. 2011. Web. 16 Feb. 2015. <http://www.centerforpubliceducation.org/Main-Menu/Organizing-a-school/Time-in-school-How-does-the-US-compare#sthash.BDP93AhK.dpuf>

Staying Informed and Involved

Parents should be actively engaged in their child's schooling and educational career. As parents you should expect to take a front-seat role in your child's education. Your student's success hinges on the active involvement of their teachers, parents, and school staff. Parents should know what content areas will be covered throughout the school year, what classes their child should be and are taking, and at the least the names of their child's teachers. Some parents go the entire year not knowing the names of their child's teachers, let along the teacher's expectations of their child. There is no reason that this should be the case.

If you find it difficult to find time to physically meet with your student's teacher(s) (which is often the largest complaint) don't give up there are various ways to stay involved and informed. Instead of waiting for quarterly progress reports, parents should monitor their student's progress every step of the way. Parents should regularly use any available streams of gaining information and keep the lines of communication open between the teacher and themselves. Parents can call, email, and in many cases send an instant message to the staff to discuss their student's progress. With so many ways to directly interact with teachers, it's easier for parents to stay in touch. At least once a week you should check in and monitor your child's progress. Establishing a routine and making this regular practice, tracking your child's academic progress should become second nature. This should be your goal.

Below I have provided five (5) tips that should help you get and stay involved and informed in your child's learning process:

1. Attend Back-to-School Night and Parent-Teacher Conferences

Attending Back-to-School Night at the start of the school year is a great way to get to know your child's teacher and his or her expectations. Here school administrators may also discuss school-wide programs and policies. Attending parent-teacher conferences throughout the academic year is another way to stay informed. These are usually held several times a year usually at progress reporting periods. The conferences are a chance to start, or continue, conversations with your child's teacher and discuss strategies to help your child do his or her best in class.

Meeting with the teacher also lets your child know that what goes on in school will be shared at home.

If your child has special learning needs, additional meetings should be scheduled with teachers and other school staff to consider setting up or revising individualized education plans (IEPs), 504 education plans, or gifted education plans.

Keep in mind that parents or guardians can request meetings (in-person or conference call) with teachers, principals, school counselors, or other school staff any time during the school year, and parents should exercise this power anytime they deem necessary.

Keep a contact log where you document the date and time of the communication, the purpose, and the agreed upon desired outcomes (action items, special requests, etc.). I cannot stress the importance enough of parents and guardians documenting everything. Efficient documentation is always easier to do if you communicate via email. Even if you speak over the phone you should send an email outlining the conversation asking the individual to respond with any questions, concerns, or found discrepancies, and confirm receipt. This should be done within 48 hours of the conversation, and do not be afraid to carbon copy (CC) or blind carbon copy (BCC) persons who you think should be privy to the information.

2. Visit the School and Its Website

Many times being visible can prevent problems before they arise. Frankly, children are less prone to misbehave and teachers are more prone to do their job. School visits also give you the opportunity to meet your child's friends and other staff members in the school besides your child's teacher. These visits also help you to learn the school's layout. Knowing the physical layout of the school building and grounds can help you connect with your child when you talk about the school day. It's good to know the location of the main office, school nurse, cafeteria, gym, athletic fields, playgrounds, auditorium, and special classes. On the school website, you should be able to find information about:

- the school calendar
- staff contact information
- upcoming events
- testing dates

Many teachers maintain their own websites that detail homework assignments, test dates, and classroom events and trips. Special resources for parents and students are also usually available on the district, school, or teacher websites. If they don't have a website, don't be afraid to ask them if they would be open to create one. You could even offer to help them with it if you are able.

3. Know the Disciplinary Policies

Schools usually cite their disciplinary policies (sometimes called the student code of conduct) in student handbooks. The rules cover expectations, and consequences for not meeting the expectations, for things like student behavior, dress codes, use of electronic devices, and acceptable language. The policies may include details about attendance, vandalism, cheating, fighting, and weapons. Many schools also have specific policies about bullying. It's helpful to know the school's definition of bullying, consequences for bullies, support for victims, and procedures for reporting bullying.

Overall, it's important for your child to know what's expected at school and that you'll support the school's consequences when expectations aren't met. It's easiest for students when school expectations match the ones at home, so children see both environments as safe and caring places that work together as a team.

4. Get Involved

Whether children are just starting kindergarten or entering their last year of high school, there are many good reasons for parents to volunteer at school. It's a great way for parents to show they're interested in their child's education. Children like to see their parents at school or at school events. However, be cognizant and follow your child's cues to find out how much interaction works for both of you. If your child seems uncomfortable with your presence at the school or with your involvement in an extracurricular activity, consider taking a more behind-the-scenes approach. Make it clear that you aren't there to intimidate them — you're just trying to help out the school community.

Parents can get involved at school by:

- being a classroom helper or homeroom parent
- organizing and/or working at fundraising activities and other special events, like assemblies, sports events, car washes, and book fairs
- chaperoning field trips
- planning class parties
- attending school board meetings
- joining the school's parent-teacher group
- working as a library assistant
- reading a story to the class
- giving a talk for career day
- attending school concerts or plays

Check the school or teacher website to find volunteer opportunities that fit your schedule. Even giving a few hours during the school year can make an impression on your child and the school staff.

5. Make Time to Talk About School

It's usually easy to talk with elementary students about what's going on in class and the latest news at school. You probably know what books your child is reading and are familiar with the math being worked on. But parents can get busy and forget to ask the simple questions, which can have an effect on children's success at school.
Make time to talk with your child every day, so he or she knows that what goes on at school is important to you. When children know parents are interested in their academic lives, they'll take school seriously as well.

Because communication is a two-way street, the way you talk and listen to your child can influence how well your child listens and responds. It's important to listen carefully, make eye contact, and avoid multitasking while you chat. Be sure to ask questions that go beyond "yes" or "no" answers. Besides during family meals, good times to talk include car trips (though eye contact isn't needed here, of course), walking the dog, preparing meals, or standing in line at a store.

STANDARDS AND CURRICULUM

The first thing parents should request from their student's teacher is a copy of the standards, information about the curriculum that they will be using, and the curriculum map for the class. These resources have proven to be essential to parent's success with "keeping up" with and providing the reinforcement needed for their child's progress throughout the academic year. When a parent has an understanding of the standards expected to be met, is familiar with the curriculum, and knows when the teacher is teaching what, they are better equipped to assist their student.

Standards

All effective educational programs build their expectations and curriculum on an adopted set of standards. All requirements for the classes offered are usually based on these standards. Thus, its essential for parents and students to understand the standards that they are expected to meet. This is typical for teachers, but many times parents are not knowledgeable of the adopted standards and if they are, they have trouble understanding them.

Standards outline what students are expected to learn in each grade and each subject. Each State Department of Education adopts or develops standards for the public schools within the state. However, private schools are at liberty to adopt or create standards of their choice. These standards become the basis for the way teachers are trained, what they teach your child(ren) and what is on state standardized tests that students must pass at the end of the academic year.

Some schools conduct a meeting with parents where they explain the standards. If this process seems foreign to you, ask your student's teacher or school administration if they plan to conduct such a meeting. If they don't, it would be in your best interest to ask them to do so. If it does not occur, parents should schedule a meeting with your child's teacher(s) with the intention of leaving with a complete understanding of the standards. Parents should also take it upon themselves to research the standards. Most state and national standards can be found online. There are even documents, presentations, and videos created specifically for the explanation of the standards.

As outlined in previous chapters, organization and positive role modeling of organized behavior speaks wonders to your child's development and adherence to your expectations. As you learn about standards and curriculum, this is a great time to exercise and sharpen your organizational skills.

Parents should create a binder where they keep a printed version of the standards along with other important documents regarding their student's academic performance. I have found it to be effective for parents to find or create a checklist of the standards (summarized) for each content area and use it to conduct frequent check-ins with their child. This will ensure that the student is successfully progressing through the curriculum.

This type of data collection can be helpful if you find yourself having issues with the teacher or curriculum effectiveness. You can bring it to your parent teacher conferences as a system of check and balance. I have seen this be extremely helpful in parent and teacher efforts to find effective academic strategies for the student, and have seen it save children from being mis-educated at the hands of an ineffective teacher. The key is for parents to be familiar with and understand the standards for themselves. This will keep parents from blindly trusting their child's educational program, something parents should never do.

Curriculum

It is very beneficial for parents to be familiar and involved with the development of the curriculum that will be taught to their children throughout the school year. The chosen curriculum will ultimately teach the child content that is to be held as truth.

Curriculum refers to the means and materials (books, worksheets, videos, etc.) with which students will interact for the purpose of meeting and/or exceeding the adopted standards. Curriculum also consists of all the planned and unplanned experiences (field trips, assemblies, guest speakers, etc.) that the school offers as part of its educational responsibility. In its most simple, essential, commonly understood form, curriculum is the "what" of education. It is crucial to academic performance and essential to culturally responsive pedagogy. The "standard" curriculum decides whose history is worthy of study, whose books are worthy of reading, which curriculum and text selections that include myriad voices and multiple ways of knowing, experiencing, and understanding life. Curriculum can help students to find and value their own voices, histories, and cultures or discount them.

My skepticism of most curricula stems from the fact that I know that many commonly used curricula are not culturally relevant. As an Urban Education specialist I know how this can be a detriment to the intellectual development of many students across the nation. A curriculum that is not culturally relevant neglects to include the culture, history, worldview, and viewpoints of the students.

Because most curriculums used in public schools are not culturally relevant, students become disengaged and many times are mis-educated. Therefore a parent knowledgeable of and contributive to the curriculum is pivotal to the child's success. I make it a point to sit down and talk to my child about what he is learning in school. There have been times when I have disagreed with the perspective of the content he was learning. Because I took the time to ask questions, I was able to contribute to the conversation and direct his perspective in the manner that I felt properly represented his culture and history.

My suggestion to parents is to be clear about what you would like your child to learn in all of the content areas, especially history (cultural, state, and world). This will help your child shape their perception of the world in a way that will benefit them and help them figure out their purpose.

Below I have provided some tips that can help you make sure your child is receiving the education that best benefits them:

1. Purchase books and workbooks that are culturally relevant and that will educate them in the manner that you feel is most beneficial. For example, knowing that the most commonly used history curriculum in America is from a European perspective and often discounts African history, as the parent of an Afrikan child, you should purchase and keep Afrikan history books and literature in your family library to share with your child. Make it a point to take some time out each week to read from these books and have intentional dialogue.

2. Plan family trips that will provide opportunities for your child to participate in activities that reinforce and/or extend the content knowledge that you would like them to attain. For example, if you are interested in your child learning STEM (Science, Technology, Engineering, and Math) instruction but the school does not offer it, find organizations that offer this instruction as extracurricular activities. Many times you may be able to find opportunities that are free of charge. Teachers and counselors are often times regularly informed about these opportunities. Ask your child's teacher and/or school counselor to keep you informed as they are.

3. Often times the school curriculum only teaches general content-based knowledge and some topics, like religion, are left out all together. Many times it is up to the parents to expose their child to in-depth information and conversations around the topics taught. One way to do this is by attending educational lectures and events with your child. For example, many local universities offer lectures series where distinguished speakers come out and do book talks or film

premiers that address important educational or social topics and/or issues that may or may not be covered in school.

4. Teach your child how to engage in self-study. When your child has questions about the content that they are learning in school or just for the heck of it, show your child how to research the topic on their own. This will not only expose them to more in-depth information around the topic, but also will also expose them to any found discrepancies and allot the opportunity for clarity.

BUILDING YOUR COMMUNITY

There was a time when people knew everyone in their community. They knew who their neighbors were, their school teachers lived amongst them, doctors and preachers were right next door, the family who owned the corner store was well known, and everyone was involved in the advancement of their community. This close-knit group knew each other well. Through constant interaction, members of the community recognized what each family stood for, believed in, expected, and even what issues they suffered with. This level of interaction ultimately fostered communal relationships between families where people felt comfortable supporting each other in their time of need.

These former communities fostered healthier environments to raise children. Neighbors or teachers would be so in tune with family expectations and child needs that they would step in and provide support. Parents would be appreciative but expect nothing less from their fellow community members because they would do the same. If parents were running late getting home, the neighbor would let the child(ren) wait inside of their home until parents arrived. If you were hungry, the owners of the corner store would let you come in and clean up to earn a bite to eat. We trusted each other. We cared for each other, and we certainly loved the children. We genuinely embodied the proverb, "It takes a village to raise a child". We must get back to this. This type of community was pivotal in successfully rearing children for the same reason it is today; rearing children is a tedious and expensive task.

This type of community is no longer a prevalent reality today. After the civil rights movement, our communities began to drastically disintegrate. Many blacks moved out of their communities and took their businesses or personal contributions to the community with them. This shift became a trend and now it is quite common for one not to know their neighbor, much less the owner of the corner store, the teachers, the doctors, or anyone in the 'community' for that matter. The village has become merely houses with people inhabiting them. Our neighbors have become mere strangers, people we train our children to stay away from. The concept of building relationships with "strangers" has become more and more discouraged, especially to our children. The village is no more, in most cases, and the loss of the strength our communities once possessed is great.

The loss of our communities has virtually eliminated the concept of individuals contributing as members of a whole. We have become individualists with individual values, individual goals, individual expectations, and individual desires with no concept of, or even seeing the necessity for, building a community. If it's not about business, money, or doesn't have any direct effect on the individual, it is none of anyone else's concern. Instead of hearing, "It takes a village to raise a child" we now hear, "You do you and I'll do me" all while our community suffers. We will watch a child go down the wrong road and not say a word out of the fear the child or parent may take offense. We then find ourselves, years later, sitting around and swapping stories of the boy down the street being in and out of trouble with the law, dropping out of school, breaking into the neighbor's house, or being shot and killed by another boy from the neighborhood "across the tracks". With a stronger sense of community, including accepting the responsibility and support that it takes to build and sustain such a group, we would have the chance to shape a more positive and productive future for our children.

A strong community provides the reinforcement needed to maintain the moral and cultural fabric of a people, and combat threats to the sustainability of that community. A strong community protects the people from destructive influences that jeopardize the well being of the village. Since we are losing our "natural community" we must make an intentional effort to build what I call our own "personal community". I came up with this concept after attending an entrepreneurial leadership conference where one of the presenters proposed that everyone should have their own personal Board of Executives (experts in their respective fields who they can consult with and depend on to give them sound advice and even support them in time of needs). I thought this was a brilliant concept. Then I began to think about how this is similar to the benefits families receive by having their own personal community to depend on.

A personal community can include friends, family, church members, colleagues, businesses you frequent, elders you admire, organizations that you are involved with, and any other person or entity that is a part of your life and reinforces and support your morals, values, and expectations. To build this community parents must be intentional in their selection of the people and entities that become a part of their and their child's lives. The people you have around you and the activities you involve yourself with have the potential to either build or destroy your family's progress. You become a product of your environment. If your environment (your community, the people around you, the places you go, the activities you are involved in) is negative and does not add value to your life, or reinforce your morals and values, then you may begin exhibiting uncharacteristic behavior, disregarding your morals and values.

Building a strong positive personal community can be done in many ways, including:

- make it a point to become involved with organization that reinforce your values,
- spend more time with friends and family members who value and support you,
- get to know the owners and patrons of some of the businesses you frequent,
- make an effort to build relationships with your child's teachers, or
- become a part of a small community known to embody your concept of community.

However you decide to accomplish this task, it is important that you consider both your and your child's needs. Your personal community should provide the support that you need to survive and you should feel comfortable doing all that you could to reciprocate that support for the community you join/create.

COMMUNITY SERVICE

One of the main reasons we no longer have communities is because we have become so spread out and isolated from each other. Organizations and communities are only sustained when the people who support them are sustained. We can actively work toward building communities by committing to support (with time and money) at least one community service event per month and encourage others to do the same. This can be a community service event that has already been established by a local church, community, school, or organization, or it can be an event you establish. The event should address the needs of the respective community and should be something that you are passionate about. Parents can also make it a point to have their child participate in the event as well.

This is a prime time for parents to reinforce morals, principles, and values with your child(ren) regarding the role they play in the community. Amongst other benefits, seeing you and other adults passionately involved in addressing the needs of the people of your community (on a volunteer basis) will serve as a great example of what your child(ren) should value and set as a priority to maintain.

What Are the Benefits of Volunteering and Community Service?

By participating in community service projects, children develop connections with other like-minded children their age, as well as other members of the community. This will develop their interpersonal skills, teaching them how to exercise empathy and exert themselves in a positive manner. Additionally, volunteerism gives children and parents the chance to exercise their responsibility to contribute to the world around them by becoming actively involved in positive ways. Another major benefit of volunteering is the level of connection it creates to a particular community. Although progressively waning, this sense of community connectedness eventually contributes toward developing the village of support parents should seek to create.

Parents must make it a point to have dialog with their children about the importance and benefits of everyone contributing to community service. Be sure that you teach them what service is and why it is a family practice, especially since community service is often times used and portrayed as an undesirable task required for a program or mandated as punishment for legal infractions or as school disciplinary policy. Take the initiative to plan service that reinforces your ideals and contributes to your community in a way that you feel is important. Explain the problem to your child that the service project will address; be sure to provide the history behind the issue so that your child will be able to empathize with the individuals being affected. Encourage your child to express their thoughts about the issue and keep the dialog solution oriented. Doing this will give the child the opportunity to exercise their critical thinking skills around the issue. Imagine the progression we can make as a people if everyone was raised, and raised their children, to be as concerned with their community as they are with themselves.

To spark your initial service project, parents can simply reach out to local organizations for their calendar of community service events planned for the quarter or year, or parents can partner with friends and family to plan your own initiative. There are plenty ideas and resources available online that will help you plan, solicit help, and implement service events. There are a plethora of organizations willing to support great service projects with resources, money, volunteers, materials, food, etc. Below I have provided some examples of community service events that are good for adults and children to participate in:

Community Service Project Suggestions

- Community Clean Up Day - Organizations plan clean up days regularly. Reach out to local organizations to see if they have any planned. If not, don't be afraid to take the initiative to start one on your own. Find a community that can use some love, solicit volunteers to support, plan your tasks for the day (i.e. rake, pick up trash, clean up overgrown weeds, paint over graffiti, etc.), pass out fliers in advance informing the community about the initiative, then get to cleaning. Community organizations (and some business) are often open to participating in initiatives like this because it directly benefits them.

- Fun Day at the nearest park - This is a great way to get everyone in the community out to commune and meet each other. This type of service is simple to organize. (1) Choose a park, (2) solicit help by passing out fliers, (3) reach out to local small businesses for support, (4) post signs informing the community of the event time, purpose and activities, (5) then have fun! This can be done in your immediate community or another community you have a connection with.

- Plan a fundraiser to raise money for a good cause. Identify a cause that you would like to support AND that will benefit the community. Plan the fundraiser with your child that will provide the funds needed to support the initiative/group/individual. You can participate in or plan a car wash, concession stand, or even host a poetry night. The key is to know exactly what you will be supporting with the monies raised and be sure to use it for that reason and that reason only. With the overabundance of fundraisers in all communities, people have to be able to trust that you are doing this for a legitimate reason and that the money will be used accordingly.

- Help elders in the community to paint and repair their homes. This will not only benefit the elder by providing the help that could possibly cost them hundreds, if not thousands of dollars, but it will benefit your family by helping you to identify and develop relationships with elders who possess the wisdom of the community. These elders could possibly end up teaching your child some of the most valuable lessons they will ever learn. It will also help build the esteem of the elders and encourage them to stay involved, something desperately needed in our community.

CHOOSING ORGANIZATIONS TO JOIN

We must make an effort to build our own personal community for our families and ourselves. This can be done in many ways, including seeking out and joining organizations that reinforce your family's mission and vision. Joining an organization will not only provide the organization the support they need, but it will also provide another opportunity for you and your child to meet like-minded individuals and grow your network of support i.e. your own personal community.

The support you and your family provide the organization will establish the support system organizations need to survive. Something that was lost when our communities became so separated. As an educator and parent I have found that there are organizations that address almost every need communities could express. When considering an organization to join or become involved with, parents should keep their morals, values, and goals in mind. Consider what you are looking to gain, and what you will be willing and able to give.

One of my main concerns as a single mother of a son was that my son wouldn't have the much-needed, consistent male influence in his life. I began to look for male involvement programs in my area. During my search I found organizations that catered to almost any need that you may have as a parent. Amongst others, I decided to join or become involve with an organization I found that had a focus in male involvement, fitness, and self-defense. I knew that I was looking for (1) good, strong, masculine, male role models, (2) an organization that reinforced my moral standards and worldview, and (3) one that would teach my son the importance of health and fitness. I was fortunate enough to find one that addressed all of them.

Before I allowed my son to become involved with the program I met all individuals involved in the program (founder, director, and instructors). I asked about their mission and vision for the program and their background (don't be afraid to ask to see their degrees or certifications if applicable). I also signed up to volunteer so that I could get to know them and their organization better, and work alongside each other.

The process of getting to know the instructors and staff was essential because you must make sure that you are placing your child in a safe environment that reinforces your expectations of your child. **Never sign your child up for a program just from reading a pamphlet or viewing a website, and never sign them up and make it a habit to just drop them off and leave.** There have been many times when I have stumbled upon wonderful websites or advertisement literature, but when I went to check the organization out they didn't quite fit the bill.

The following are the steps I take when choosing organizations that my son and I will become involved with:

1. Google the organization name, you never know what will come up.

2. If nothing negative is found, check out their mission statement.

3. Find the names of the Founder/Program Director and support staff and Google their names.

4. If nothing negative is found, call to schedule an appointment with the Program Director or Program Coordinator to discuss the possibility of joining and supporting the organization. During this meeting mission, vision, and goals on both ends are discussed.

5. If all goes well, I join and support the program on a trial basis carefully looking out for any red flags.

Special care is absolutely necessary in this day and age, especially since history has shown that individuals who have a desire to abuse children seek to work at and/or hang around organizations that serve children. Additionally, I have found that some adults who work with children in schools and organization do not behave appropriately and have ideals and biases that are projected on the children, which in many cases negatively impact the children. This is why it is important for parents to be actively involved with any organization that their child is involved with. I suggest that parents take about 4-8 weeks to really get to know the organization and the staff. This will give the chance for "true colors" to show themselves and decrease the risk of you becoming involved with an organization that does not fit your family's standards.

Once a suitable organization is found be sure that you honor your commitment to support and participate in the program. Schedule times to volunteer, participate in fundraisers, give what you can when you can, spread the word about the work the organization is doing, and solicit support when the opportunity presents itself. The more you support the organization, the stronger the relationship your family will build with the organization.

In most cases, organizations take very good care of their participants who support them. It's all about reciprocation. Give what you would like to get out of the organization. Remember the people who you meet and begin to forge relationships with will become your own personal community whom hopefully you can lean and depend if you ever find yourself in need.

CONCLUSION

It has been my attempt to provide you with practical and empowering strategies to help rear your child and unleash the genius in them. The key thing to remember is that your child is a genius and it's up to the adult(s) around them to facilitate their learning, support them, protect them (uncompromisingly), nurture them, and encourage them to know and love themselves. By making strategic and consistent efforts to take greater control of their environment and influences, your child will be better equipped with the confidence and knowhow needed to accomplish what they will.

Be confident that you are more than capable to rear them well. Never give up when times get hard and never hesitate to solicit support from the friends, family, and community whom you trust. Continue to take your responsibility to rear them well seriously and be proudly uncompromising when it comes to upholding your mission, values, goals, standards, and expectations. Also, don't be afraid to hold all who are involved in you and your child's life accountable as well. Let them know what your expectations are and explain to them that you will not compromise and that you will do all that you can to protect your child.

This book would not be complete if I didn't share additional resources that have been extremely effective in my growth as a parent; resources I think all parents, families, and communities of Afrikan children should always have accessible. Below you will find a list of books and names of scholars that I think are beneficial for you to become familiar with. The books are easily accessible for purchase online and many of the scholars also have articles, papers and videos of their lectures online. Remember to stay the course and know that you have already taken the first steps toward rearing your child well by recognizing you, as a parent, possess the power to make the greatest impact in their life.

Suggested Books

SBA: The Reawakening of the African Mind, Dr. Asa G. Hilliard, III

The Maroon Within Us, Dr. Asa G. Hilliard, III

The Teachings of Ptahhotep: The Oldest Book in the World, Dr. Asa G. Hilliard, III, Larry Williams, Nia Damali

Young Gifted and Black, Theresa Perry, Claude Steele, and Dr. Asa G. Hilliard, III

Nile Valley Contributions to Civilization (Book and Study Guide), Anthony Browder

IWA: A Warrior's Character, Mwalimu K. Bomani Baruti

Brainwashed: Challenging the Myth of Black Inferiority, Tom Burrell

The New Jim Crow, Michelle Alexander

The Destruction of Black Civilization: Great Issues of a Race from 4500 B.C. to 2000 A.D., Chancellor Williams

The Mis-Education of the Negro, Carter G. Woodson

Dick Gregory's Natural Diet for Folks Who Eat: Cookin' with Mother Nature, Dick Gregory

Awakening the Natural Genius of Black Children, Amos Wilson

Scholars To Study

Dr. Amos Wilson

Dr. Asa G. Hilliard, III

Dr. Claude Anderson

Dr. Frances Cress Welsing

Dr. Kobi Kambon

Malcolm X

Michelle Alexander

Mwalimu K. Bomani Baruti

Dr. Wade Nobles